Corpse!

A comedy thriller

Gerald Moon

Samuel French—London
New York—Sydney—Toronto—Hollywood

CORPSE!

The play was presented by Robert Fox Limited and Gary Leaverton in association with Michael Medwin for Memorial Films and EEE Inc at the Apollo Theatre, London, on 26th July 1984, with the following cast:

Evelyn Farrant	Keith Baxter
Mrs McGee	Joyce Grant
Major Ambrose Powell	Milo O'Shea
Rupert Farrant	Keith Baxter
Hawkins	Richard Hampton

The play directed by **John Tillinger**
Designed by **Alan Tagg**

The action of the play takes place in Evelyn's basement flat in Soho, and Rupert's house in Regent's Park.

Time: December, 1936. London

Act I
  Scene 1   Evelyn's flat. Midday
  Scene 2   Rupert's flat. Seven o'clock that night
  Scene 3   Evelyn's flat. Shortly after

Act II
  Scene 1   Evelyn's flat. Immediately following
  Scene 2   Rupert's flat. A while later

AUTHOR'S NOTE

Corpse! is a Comedy Thriller and in all advertising and publicity no description other than 'Comedy Thriller' may be used.

G.M.

PRODUCTION NOTE

This Acting Edition is based on the production of the play in London's West End, where two sets were used as the theatre concerned was equipped with a revolve. The play has been equally successfully produced in America with the settings placed side by side, and a ground plan illustrating this can be found on page 49.

The **photographs** in this Acting Edition are by DAVID JAMES and show the settings by ALAN TAGG for the London production which are © 1984 by Alan Tagg.

This play is dedicated with love and respect to

TERRY WOOD
Royal Shakespeare Company Actor
(1948–1982)

and

RAY SARGEANT
(1946–1983)

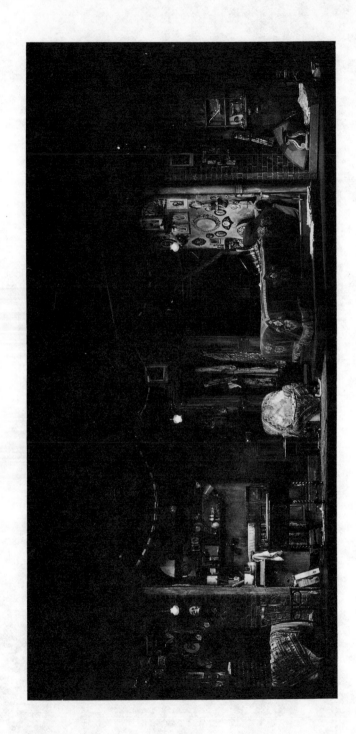

ACT I*

SCENE 1

Evelyn Farrant's basement flat in Soho, London. December 1936. Midday
The whole flat has an atmosphere of faded theatrical griminess. It is damp
and musty with stacks of old newspapers, junk and bric-a-brac scattered
around

The flat is entered from iron fire escape-type steps which come down from
street level, past a skylight and window in the back wall above the kitchen
area. The front door is in the centre of the back wall with the kitchen area
up one step R. There are pots, pans, a practical sink and practical two-ring
gas stove in the kitchen. Below this is an alcove DR in which there is a large
theatrical skip full of old costumes. On the wall adjoining the alcove and
kitchen is a gas lamp and below this a skull, containing the three "piggies"
or bullets for the gun. There is also a frame on the wall containing a photo
of Rupert

An old desk and upright chair stand downstage R with an old armchair and
table centre. The bedroom area is L, up a step, with a large bed covered by
a torn and faded bedspread

Immediately L of the front door is a walk-in cupboard full of costumes and
another, free standing, wardrobe stands in the corner UL. A torn curtain,
behind which Evelyn changes, is just above the bed

Another small alcove DL contains a stool and a small set of drawers with
make-up articles in them together with the photograph of Evelyn's "mother"

There are theatrical posters on the walls and the whole set is littered with
props—swords, goblets etc.

There are two further practical gas lamps, in addition to the one near the
kitchen. These are to the L of the front door and above the bed

There are four trick escapes from the set:
(1) under the bed and off L
(2) behind the changing curtain
(3) through cupboard by front door
(4) panel in wardrobe for swapping revolvers and taking off watch

As the CURTAIN rises London street noises are heard. Light streams in
from the window, illuminating the bedroom area. There is a moment's pause

A lady passes the skylight and comes down the stairs. Her footsteps are
heard. A key is inserted in the front door, which opens slowly. We see a

---

N.B. Paragraph 3 on p. ii of this Acting Edition regarding photocopying
and video-recording should be carefully read.

woman's figure. "She" enters the flat and closes the door. The street noises cease.

We now see Evelyn Farrant, dressed as an elegant elderly woman in the Queen Mary mould. "She" carries a large handbag and an umbrella. Evelyn totters into the room

Evelyn (*in an affected woman's voice*) My poor child. Such a place! So sinister. How could anyone live in such squalor. Here's a fine kettle of fish indeed. So depressing. Urrrgh! I see the maid hasn't been in here today. And the time ... my dear ... what is it? Heavens, five and twenty minutes past noon. *Il faut commencer la comedie* ... Much to do and not a lady-in-waiting in sight!

Mrs McGee (*off*) Hello.

Evelyn (*speaking normally*) Oh, I spoke too soon.

Mrs McGee (*off*) Evelyn ... Are you in there dear?

Evelyn There's no one at home, I'm afraid.

Mrs McGee (*off*) Don't be silly dear, let me in at once or I shall use my pass key.

Mrs McGee enters. She is middle-aged, garrulous and affected, open to flattery but anxious not to be taken advantage of

Oh, I do beg your pardon, ma'am ... sorry, I was looking for Evelyn Farrant.

Evelyn They seek him here—they seek him there, those Frenchies seek Evelyn everywhere ...

Mrs McGee Oh, Evelyn, really! You shouldn't play these naughty tricks on me. You really shouldn't. The slightest thing upsets my equilibrium. I must sit down for a minute ... (*She sits in the armchair*)

Evelyn ... do dear, take the weight off your feet ...

Mrs McGee I'm so upset anyway. I've been glued to the wireless set all day—listening to the news bulletins. He's going, you know. My King!

Evelyn Yes, it's sickening ...

Mrs McGee He's going to that awful Wallace Simpson woman.

Evelyn Well, she's American dear, what do you expect, grab, grab, grab.

Mrs McGee He's going to speak to us all on the wireless tonight. Of course, I blame his mother.

Evelyn Now, Mrs McGee dear, what do you want?

Mrs McGee I do so hate to be a nuisance, and you know how I try not to be one of those busybody landladies, but there is just the little—hurdle—of the rent.

Evelyn Oh, Mrs McGee, I do promise you most faithfully you shall have it by the end of the month.

Mrs McGee It is long overdue. Oh, Evelyn, those legs ... are they your own? And such a delicate shade of stocking. Where did you acquire them?

Evelyn sits on the desk showing off his stockings

Evelyn I searched everywhere—Liberty's, Swan and Edgars. But, as usual, it was Dickens and Jones that really understands a woman's sensibilities.
Mrs McGee You theatricals! Please—don't make me laugh. I can feel one of my excrutiating migraines coming on.
Evelyn You poor thing!
Mrs McGee Oh, but Evelyn—you haven't been walking through the West End like that, have you?
Evelyn Certainly.
Mrs McGee Were you auditioning for a pantomime dear?
Evelyn I've been to Fortnum and Mason's for lunch.
Mrs McGee Fortnums?
Evelyn It's a principle of mine, Mrs McGee. When I'm down on my uppers, I always take lunch at Fortnums!
Mrs McGee And what, pray, was on the menu today?

Evelyn opens the umbrella and a loaf of French bread falls out

Evelyn French bread ... Pâté de Foie Gras with truffles, delicious. (*He takes a pot of pâté from the inside breast pocket of his coat*) Caviare, divine. (*He again produces the caviare from his inside pocket*) And this, my dear Mrs McGee, is for you! (*He searches in his left stocking top*)
Mrs McGee No, no, I couldn't. I really couldn't. What is it?
Evelyn Gentleman's Relish! (*He hands it to her*)
Mrs McGee How nice!

Evelyn opens his coat to show bottles hanging on a harness

Evelyn Irish whiskey and a particularly fine Hock! Many hampers make light fingers!
Mrs McGee Oh, Evelyn—that's dangerous dear. You could be arrested.
Evelyn Not dressed like this I couldn't.
Mrs McGee But it's still stealing.
Evelyn Stealing! It's not stealing, it's socialism! (*He takes off his hat and crosses to the bed to undress*) Messrs Fortnum and Mason are stinking rich and Mr Evelyn Farrant is very poor. It's an equitable distribution of profit.
Mrs McGee I must say you don't look poor to me at the moment. Unless I'm much mistaken that's silver fox!

Evelyn takes his coat off and puts it carefully on the bed

Evelyn Rabbit! It's what I wore as Richard the Third when I went on for Ernest Milton. After they gave me the sack Miss Baylis said I could keep the costume because no one else would touch it. The beads ... the beads were Ellen Terry's, and the shoes, I am afraid ... Widow Twankey!

Evelyn hangs the beads over the gas fitting by the bed. The shoes go with the hat in the open hat box on the bed which then goes away up on the wardrobe

Mrs McGee Oh Evelyn, you have such lovely things, why don't you sell some of them?

Evelyn Never!

Mrs McGee Then you wouldn't have to worry about your financial embarrassment would you?

Evelyn I need them, Mrs McGee. (*Still wearing the dress, he crosses to the kitchen and polishes two goblets*)

Mrs McGee Those goblets must be worth something?

Evelyn Lyceum Theatre. "The House of Death and Blood".

Mrs McGee Oh, Evelyn, are you inviting me for a drinkie, dear?

Evelyn No, I am expecting a visitor, Mrs McGee.

Evelyn goes to the desk with the goblets and starts to tidy up. He unseals the caviare pot lid

Mrs McGee Sorry if I am a little *de trop*, dear.

Evelyn A male visitor, Mrs McGee.

Mrs McGee You know, Evelyn, I have never known a man with so many nephews!

Evelyn It's not a nephew today, Mrs McGee.

Mrs McGee Why can't it ever be a rich uncle, that's what I say.

Evelyn takes off his wig, putting it in the wig tin DL, gets face cream and removes his make-up

Evelyn Perhaps . . . it will be a godfather!

Mrs McGee A generous one, I hope. I know it's distasteful for me to have to remind you about the rent—but things aren't all that easy for a woman without a husband to support her.

Evelyn Have no fear, my Mrs McGee dear, you will receive what's coming to you in due course.

Mrs McGee There is a 'rôle' on the horizon—is that what you mean?

Evelyn It means—if I play my cards right my dear—my fortune will be made at last.

Mrs McGee But you deserve it. You really do. As I was only saying so the other day to my friend at the Foot Clinic—my Mr Farrant deserves a break. Oh, yes you do, Evelyn. A fine, handsome, talented leading man like yourself, you should have your own company of players.

Evelyn Ah Mrs McGee, that has always been my dream. (*He goes to the sink to wash*)

Mrs McGee Not that you weren't lovely as a chrysalis in that insect play . . .

Evelyn Second creepy crawler, Mrs McGee!

Mrs McGee Second crawler . . . you were so lifelike! . . . And now resting. For close on two years! It's not fair.

Mrs McGee gets up and closes in on Evelyn at the sink

You may not realise this, Evelyn, but I am terribly sensitive to artists. I feel for you. But that doesn't mean I'm going to turn a blind eye to the rent that is in abeyance.

Evelyn Of course not, dear lady . . .

Mrs McGee It's hard for all of us in these troubled times. Especially for me—since my "beloved" George passed over.

Evelyn I wish you wouldn't say "passed over", Mrs McGee dear, George died!

Mrs McGee He did pass over, dear, in a manner of speaking. Working for the Gas Board—and blowing himself up. Bits of him everywhere.

Evelyn His generosity knew no bounds.

Mrs McGee And now I'm alone. And so are you. Twin souls bobbing about on the ocean of life. That's why I value your friendship, Evelyn, I really do, it means a great deal to me. Perhaps we can come to some sort of arrangement about the rent, if you follow me.

Evelyn Yes, I follow you, dear lady—but please—time is of the essence and I must now ask you to leave.

Evelyn opens the door to usher her out

Mrs McGee I'm on my way. And—Evelyn—think it over—about an arrangement.

Mrs McGee exits, closing the door behind her

Evelyn Certainly. *Au revoir.* I think Evelyn it's time you got a move on ... Five minutes. Quickness and calm. Quickness and calm. (*He unbuttons his dress during the next speech*) I can do it, can't I ...?

> "I can add colours to the chameleon,
> Change shapes with Proteus for advantages,
> And set the murd'rous Machiavelli to school.
> Can I do this, and cannot get a crown ...?

Yes, I can. (*The dress falls, leaving him in stockings and corset*)

Mrs McGee enters carrying napkins, goes coy and hides her face in the napkins

Mrs McGee Evelyn ... oh, I don't quite know where to look. I've borrowed these napkins ... from Mrs ... my er ... friend at forty-three. Oh, such a fine figure of a man ... I think I'd better run upstairs and have a little lie down.

Mrs McGee exits

Evelyn God, if I'm not very careful that meddlesome old chatterbox could ruin the whole thing. (*He takes off the corset and stockings*) Two minutes and it's going to work isn't it? It's going to be brilliant. Brilliant. (*He throws the clothes into a skip*) It cannot be flawed. He'll be here any minute now.

Major Ambrose Powell crosses the skylight

Evelyn puts on a dressing gown and slippers from the cupboard UC

Oh look dear, what did I tell you! His timing, like mine, is perfection.

There is a knock at the door. Evelyn opens it

Major Powell is on the doorstep. He wears a coat and hat and is middle-aged, portly and Irish

Powell Good afternoon.
Evelyn Good afternoon.
Powell Is it Mr Evelyn Farrant?
Evelyn It most certainly is Mr Powell?
Powell Major. Major Powell.
Evelyn Major Powell, yes of course. Won't you come in?
Powell Thank you. (*He comes into the room*)
Evelyn May I take your hat and coat?
Powell I'll hold on to them if you don't mind. (*He moves about looking at the flat*)
Evelyn So good of you to make it. Do sit down, make yourself at home. Now first things first. How about a drink?
Powell A drink? Oh, yes, please. I shouldn't really ...
Evelyn Of course not, You live with an ulcer.
Powell How did you know?
Evelyn Whiskey? Irish?—Jameson's? Isn't that your tipple?
Powell Well ... when offered ...yes ... Yes, it is. With a splash of water.
Evelyn Water.
Powell You seem to know a lot about me.
Evelyn I most certainly do.
Powell Do you? I see. Why have you invited me here?
Evelyn Oh, we're coming to that, Brigadier Powell.
Powell Major. I'm a Major.
Evelyn Major—yes. Of course you are. Major Ambrose Walter Powell. And how very kind of you to keep the appointment. "Dead on time, too". Couldn't be better. (*He sits R of the desk*)
Powell Your letter intrigued me. And you did mention money!
Evelyn Did I?
Powell Most definitely.
Evelyn Cheers.
Powell Cheers ... oh, for the ulcer (*He takes a pill out of his pocket and puts it in his drink*)
Evelyn They make aggravating companions!
Powell Now, just exactly who are you? What are you?
Evelyn Who am I? I, sir, am an actor.
Powell Oh, one of those! (*He sits in the armchair*)
Evelyn A world unfamiliar to you, I assume, Major?
Powell Yes, it is. And I'm glad to say I don't go to the theatre.
Evelyn Then allow me to bring the theatre to you—over a little light luncheon.
Powell Oh! Lunch, of course.
Evelyn I hope you like blinis?
Powell Blinis? I've never eaten there.
Evelyn Blinis, my dear sir, are Russian pancakes—sautéed with onions, topped with sour cream and laced with caviare.
Powell Well ... er ... a boiled egg would suffice!

Evelyn prepares the food on a big chopping board on the desk

Evelyn Pâté de foie gras with truffles. A smidgeon of that for starters wouldn't you say?
Powell Sounds ... very tasty ...
Evelyn On French bread.
Powell Thank you.
Evelyn I can't offer you a dessert I'm afraid—I could not reach the stuffed peaches. And I'll open the Hock in one moment. (*He tidies the chopping board and food from the desk to the kitchen*)
Powell So you're in show business?
Evelyn Absolutely not! "I am of the theatre". (*He lights the stove with a match*)
Powell Really! And out of work, I suppose.
Evelyn I can't get work. I'm too good. They're frightened of my brilliance And then—sadly—there is this ridiculous stigma. (*He pours oil into a pan and leaves it to heat up on the stove. He then takes a small chopping board and an onion to the desk and chops the onion up*)
Powell Stigma?
Evelyn A few years ago I appeared in a play called "The Macropolous Secret". I played Jaroslav Pruss. It was common knowledge that there was bad blood between the juvenile lead and myself. Though I cannot imagine why. A few hours before the curtain rose on the first night the actor fell sick and by a surprising chance I had studied the lines and was able to take his place. I had a triumph. Unhappily the actor put it about that I had engineered the incident. There was some talk of poison. In chocolates. I never gave him chocolates. But the wretched coincidences of my fascination for curious esoteric poisons being well-known was sufficient to condemn me. The rumour was that I had administered curare. Are you familiar with this particular poison, Major?
Powell Not in my line of country. I'm relieved to say, Mr Farrant.
Evelyn No, it wouldn't be—unless your country happens to be Brazil. Curare acts upon the motor nerves and causes muscular paralysis. The pulse diminishes till it's barely perceptible.
Powell Good heavens.

Evelyn pours the chopped onions into the hot pan. They sizzle and he moves them to the second gas ring to simmer. He puts oil in the second pan for the first pancake

Evelyn I was entirely innocent of the calumny. But you know, Major, how these wicked stories spread. Along with the carriage trade, it travelled across Waterloo Bridge into the Old Vic itself and even Lilian Baylis asked me to leave when half the court of *Hamlet* went down with whooping cough! Alas, I haven't worked since!
Powell Is that so. A very tragic tale.
Evelyn Isn't it. But let us address ourselves to more cheerful matters ... Now, Major—if you agree to the terms—my forthcoming performance will enable you to earn a substantial amount of money.
Powell How much?
Evelyn Five thousand pounds.

Powell (*rising*) Five ... then tell me, Mr Farrant—what exactly do you want me to do?

Evelyn What do I want you to do? I want you—to murder me!

Powell Murder you ...

Evelyn I don't want you to murder me actually, but him! (*He points to the picture of Rupert on the wall*)

Powell But, isn't that ...

Evelyn That, sir, is my brother. My twin brother, Rupert. I want him dead!

Powell You wish your brother dead? But ... why?

Evelyn Because ... he's very rich ... and I hate him.

Powell You hate your brother so much to want to kill him?

Evelyn We are twins—and we hate one another.

Powell How unfortunate.

During his next speech Evelyn pours pancake batter into the pan and cooks the first pancake

Evelyn Isn't it. But not unique. The world is full of hate, Major. Especially in families. Do you know, Powell, everybody is under the impression that twins are devoted to each other ... inseparable. Well, we were the exception. Everybody loved Rupert. All the favours were heaped on him. The sensible one, they'd say, so graceful, so elegant,—so insufferably polite. They were all fooled. All of them. I was the only one who knew that underneath he was cold ... calculating ... Please, do sit down.

Powell Thank you.

Evelyn My darling mother was a great beauty as a young girl. She fell in love with an adventurer. And though her parents disapproved, so great was her obsession that she ran away with him. Disowned by her family and abandoned by her lover when he discovered that she was penniless and pregnant. My darling mother almost starved to bring us up.

Powell Do you mean your father abandoned you—?

Evelyn Before we were born.

Powell I should have thought he'd be the one you'd want to kill!

Evelyn Very true.

Powell What happened to him?

Evelyn "Daddy's dead"—that's what Rupert used to say. "Daddy's dead and buried". It was typical of Rupert. He was always tormenting me. Tying me up in the broom cupboard—for hours on end—in the dark! Breaking windows and telling everyone that I'd done it. And they always believed him. Never me. And nothing I ever did was good enough—however hard I tried. He was always top of the class. Head Prefect. Brilliant at games. His name emblazoned in letters of gold on the school honours board. A spiffing all-rounder! And I couldn't get into the cricket eleven! (*He tosses the first pancake then puts it on a plate over the onions to keep warm*)

Powell Oh, dear. How sad.

Evelyn And so it continued until my mother married.

Powell Ah—Mr Farrant?

Evelyn begins cooking the second pancake, without oil

Evelyn Absolutely not! Mother gave Rupert and me the name of Farrant. Step-father's name was Brewer. I would certainly never have used that name professionally. It would look decidedly cheap on the bill-boards. Don't you agree? Evelyn Brewer. And *he* adored Rupert. He idolized him. I might just as well never have existed.

Powell Well, at least you had your Mummy to turn to.

Evelyn She was so captivated by Mr Brewer she had little enough time for me any more. I saw how it was. I forgave her. I would have forgiven her anything—even when she handed over to my step-father the little inheritance she received at her parents' death. Brewer took that money, Powell—it was the foundation of all his fortune. My darling mother had nothing to bequeath me when she died. I was so overwhelmed with grief—what was money to me then. I lost the only person who really appreciated my talent. But when *he* died—he left everything to Rupert ... the house ... the money ... the business ... everything. I wasn't even mentioned in the will. And I'm the oldest, Major Powell—by five whole minutes. And now the time has come to claim what is rightfully mine ... and because of that ... Rupert Farrant ... whom everybody loves ... must die! (*He tosses the second pancake*)

Powell How are you going to kill him?

Evelyn Correction. How are *you* going to kill him. It's quite simple: you go to Rupert and persuade him to come here tonight. You tell him you are a friend and that I am dying.

Powell What of?

Evelyn (*drinking from his goblet*) Cirrhosis of the liver. Cheers!

Powell Nasty!

Evelyn He comes here—and you shoot him. I shall leave a suicide note from "me" to "him". Once he is dead—he becomes me—and I become him!

Powell Please ... let me grasp exactly what you've said: when he is dead— "he" becomes "you" and "you" become "him". Is that right?

Evelyn That's it exactly.

Powell goes to the front door, preparing to exit

Powell I'm sorry—I wouldn't do it if you were to offer me ten thousand pounds.

Evelyn Very well. Ten thousand pounds it is. In cash. Within the month. And with Jameson's at twelve bob a bottle—that's a lot of whiskey, Major!

Powell Ten thousand pounds.

Evelyn I've already told you—Rupert's very rich.

Powell How can I be sure I'd get the money?

Evelyn Oh, you'll get it. I won't double-cross you.

Powell How do I know you won't double-cross me?

Evelyn How do I know you won't double-cross *me*?

Powell Why would I double-cross you? I need the money.

Evelyn Why would I double-cross you—*I* need the money!

Powell (*taking off his raincoat*) Ten thousand pounds.

Evelyn Doesn't fall into your lap every day, now does it? (*He sets cutlery on the table*)

Powell No, no it certainly doesn't.

Evelyn Ten thousand pounds ...

Powell In cash.

Evelyn Within the month. Do sit down.

Powell Thank you.

Evelyn Sounds good doesn't it?

Powell (*crossing to sit down*) Yes.

Evelyn Have a blini. Smother it with onions. Drown it in sour cream. Be lavish with the caviare. (*He prepares a blini for Powell*)

Powell Most kind. Er—thank you—that's enough!

Evelyn Bon appetit!

Powell No thank you—no mustard. (*He tastes his blini and finds it disgusting*)

Evelyn prepares his own food whistling "You Do Something To Me!"

(*After a while*) Ten thousand pounds ...

Evelyn Sounds better every time you say it.

Powell Well—I mean to say ... A sum like that! Funds rather low just now. Meagre pension. Been difficult to settle down—

Evelyn (*opening the wine*) Yes, you have been rather on the move haven't you?

Powell No place for an old soldier to lay his head. I've been abroad you know. Had to get away from this climate—

Evelyn Too hot for you was it?

Powell I beg your pardon.

Evelyn (*pouring the wine*) Cheers.

Powell Cheers. (*He drinks*) So I decided to depart these shores.

Evelyn To escape, in other words.

Powell Well, yes.

Evelyn To the United States of America. Philadelphia, and then back to Canada where you were before the war.

Powell One has to live you know.

Evelyn Seventy eight addresses in the last two years! And now you're back in London—holed up in Paddington. Hotel Tavistock, top floor, room eleven, one light bulb no soap! and a very small suitcase! On the run again, this time from Eddie Chan.

Powell Eddie Chan! (*He drops his knife and fork and rises in fear*)

Evelyn He's looking for you, Major. You shot his brother down in Limehouse.

Powell Are you part of the Eddie Chan mob?

Evelyn I am in no way connected with that organization, Major.

Powell Thank God for that!

Evelyn Beyond the fact that one of Mr Chan's boys is a particular friend of mine.

Powell And what the hell does that mean?

Evelyn Never mind dear! Oh, this is delicious, isn't it? The point is I am offering you sufficient funds to keep you to the end of your days. You'll be secure. For the first time in your life. No more running. Questions.

Powell Assuming I say "yes"—how can I be sure I won't be implicated?

Evelyn In what way?

Powell Supposing someone happens to see me entering or leaving this building?

Evelyn They won't if you follow my orders. My landlady, Mrs McGee, spends every Friday night at number forty-three. So the house will be empty.

Powell What about out in the street?

Evelyn The whole of London, Major, will be huddled over their wireless sets.

Powell You mean listening to the King's broadcast?

Evelyn Exactly! It could not be more perfect. In any case—I shall be your alibi. If the police suspect foul play and question your whereabouts—which they won't—I, as Rupert by then, will tell them that you spent the evening with me.

Powell Clever.

Evelyn Isn't it! You see, dear Major, you'll find that every detail had been worked out.

Powell When your brother comes here—who opens the door?

Evelyn He does. With key. From me. You'll give it to him.

Powell I see. And—tell me—will you be here?

Evelyn Oh no, Major. You will be, though—to murder me!

Powell Now wait a moment. I haven't agreed to do it yet. In any case.... I could go to the police.

Evelyn The police! With your history! You are so well known to Scotland Yard, you must be the only civilian to receive free tickets to the Policeman's Ball!

Powell I've often been questioned. I've never been charged.

Evelyn Always a bridesmaid—and never a bride, eh? (*He takes the dirty plates to the sink*) Oh look, you've hardly touched your blini ...

Powell It tasted sort of fishy ...

Evelyn "Caviare to the General!"

Powell Major!

Evelyn Major! (*Taking a folder from the desk drawer*) It's all in there.

Powell What's this?

Evelyn A complete dossier on Rupert Farrant. Everything—everything—I need to know about my brother. I know the names of his bank manager, his dentist—and need I add, his lawyer. I know his habits, how he moves, how he tells a joke. I really must practise mis-timing. And I know the names of all his women ... I'm delightfully acquainted with his tastes ... sexually. Thank God I'm versatile!

Powell (*looking through the folder*) Good heavens! You haven't left anything to chance, have you?

Evelyn Chance is for gamblers, Major. The stakes are too high to gamble.

Evelyn crosses to the bedroom and disappears behind the curtain to change

Powell Are they indeed! (*Flicking through the folder*) "Sports. A fencing man." I did a bit of that at school myself. "Golf. Swimming. Squash. Riding. To be seen in the Royal Enclosure at Ascot." How nice. "Artists and Painting. Manet. Especially admires Van Gogh (*pronounces it as "Go"*) early pen and ink sketches. (*He turns the page*) Music ... music ... music ... (*turns page*) Rupert Farrant, Sexual." (*Turns page*) "Rupert Farrant, Fi" ... (*turns back the page*) I've never heard of that. You'd have to be very fit. Heavens—he must be quite the ladies man, eh, Mr Farrant? Ah! The ladies! You know—they will be my downfall. Convinced of it. But then—it was the only talent I've ever possessed.

Evelyn (*off*) Talent?

Powell Talent. Charm. Oh, believe me—you'd be surprised how quickly ladies have always succumbed to my looks and my old-fashioned way. And with the suggestion of the possibility of a little—how shall we put it—a little "hanky-panky" on the side, they were delighted to hand over enormous sums of money. But, of course, not quite ten thousand pounds! (*He spies the blini on his plate, looks across to the curtain, grabs the plate and hides it in the cupboard under the stove*) But—murder—Mr Farrant. I mean to say an officer and a gentleman doesn't commit murder.

Evelyn (*off*) Gentleman?

Powell I got into the Army. Became an Officer. Mons. Ypres. The Somme. It was terrible. (*His eye catches the pearls Evelyn wore as the "Lady". He crosses to the gas lamp above the bed*) Major Powell of the Grenadier Guards. Promoted on the field at Mons. (*He is about to take the pearls*)

Evelyn (*off*) Demoted on the field, you mean!

Powell's hand darts behind his back. A moment—then he steals the pearls

Powell I was at Mons. (*He moves away with the pearls in his pocket*)

Evelyn's head appears from behind the curtain

Evelyn I know you were, dear. Skulking behind the front lines. Racketeering in damp cigarettes, watered whisky and used girls!

Evelyn's head disappears again

Powell Well, damn it, one has to live, you know! Things were very difficult after the war. I was on the point of leaving for the Indian Civil Service, when I was caught in a compromising situation—with the Archdeacon's wife ... in the vestry ... during Epiphany. (*He holds the pearls up to the light to see if they are real*)

Evelyn enters. He has completely changed and is now dressed as "Rupert", wearing a smart blue pin-stripe suit, black shoes, white shirt and tie, hair neatly combed and spectacles. He carries a revolver and takes aim at Powell

Evelyn Put down those pearls, Major.

Powell I was just admiring them. (*He sees the gun aimed at him*) No ... No ... No ....

Evelyn fires the gun and Powell falls backwards into the open skip. A long moment. Then Powell stirs

Powell What the hell are you playing at, you bloody fool!

Evelyn A blank, Major. Next time it will be a "live" performance.

Evelyn assists Powell out of the skip, takes the pearls, crosses back to the gas lamp at the bed and re-hangs them

Paste—but priceless!

Powell Bloody actors! If I had any idea I was going to be used as target practise, I would have brought along my riding crop and whipped the skin off your back!

Evelyn screams at Powell and aims the gun again. Powell flinches

Evelyn Major Ambrose Walter Powell—of the Tipperary Irregulars! Embezzeler! Forger! Pickpocket! Thief! "The snapper up of unconsidered trifles!"

Powell Damn you! You put the fear of God in me.

Evelyn (*calmer*) Yes. I meant to. Do help yourself to another drink—you look as if you need it.

Powell Thank you. (*He swigs from the bottle*)

Evelyn Well, this should be a simple enough assignment for you, Major. What was it they called you in the Army—"One Shot Wally?"

Powell I always had a good eye, you know. Yes—"One Shot Wally". I was rather proud of that.

Evelyn Let us see if your eye is still in, my dear sir, because one shot is all you're going to get.

Powell You mean fire the gun again ...

Evelyn Certainly.

Powell What about the landlady?

Evelyn She will be comatose on the cooking sherry by now, Major.

Powell But—what at?

Evelyn points to the framed photo of Rupert on the wall above the stove

Evelyn Rupert—of course

Powell looks at the photo closely—then back to Evelyn

Powell My God! That is uncanny.

Evelyn "For one of us was born a twin—
And not a soul knew which. ...."

Powell Quite amazing. Your brother looks....

Evelyn Successful. Suave. And he is utterly ruthless. Unlike his brother who is just an innocent bundle of fun. (*He offers the gun to Powell*) You simply—aim and fire!

Powell That's too easy.

Evelyn Really? Then turn your back.

Powell All right. (*He turns his back*)

Evelyn Fire on the count of three. One ... Two ... (*He moves out of firing range to the front door and stares at the photo*) Three.

Powell turns and aims and fires at the frame. It smashes

I'm impressed. You would have blown his head right off!

Powell One Shot Wally always scores a bull's eye. Shall I hit him between the eyes?

Evelyn Absolutely not. It's perverse of me I know but when he's laid out as the dead Evelyn I want to savour the tributes to my beauty. Aim for the heart! If you can find it! Safer in here, don't you think? (*He puts the gun in the desk drawer*)

Powell Where does he live?

Evelyn Rupert? Number one hundred and fourteen Connaught Terrace. Overlooking Regent's Park. From here, ten minutes by cab.

Powell What's his house like?

Evelyn I've never been allowed across the threshold.

Powell How do I know he'll be there?

Evelyn Oh, he'll be there all right. It's Friday. He runs his life most meticulously. It's as dull as clockwork! At four thirty he has a fencing session with Giles St Regis. He will return home to change before dining with Sir Bertram Nesbitt at the Berkeley. Sir Bertram is Rupert's solicitor and financial adviser. Every Friday they dine together to discuss the manipulation of Rupert's mounting fortune (*He puts the folder away in the desk and puts on a gold watch*)

Powell What about servants? Does he have those?

Evelyn A cook and a butler, Mr and Mrs Hammond, are away for the Christmas holidays. So he'll be alone.

Powell But why does it have to be tonight? What's the hurry?

Evelyn He's leaving for Scotland tomorrow. It's in the "News Chronicle".

Evelyn crosses to the bed to get the newspaper, bumping into Powell on the way. This is where Powell "steals" Evelyn's watch. In reality there are two watches, one already in Powell's pocket

Ah, here we are ... "The marriage between up-and-coming financier Mr Rupert Farrant and the lovely Lady Moira Graeme, aged twenty-two, will take place at the Private Chapel of Drumnadrochit Castle on December seventeenth." Charming, isn't it?

Powell Listen—I've got a smashing idea: Why don't you wait till after he's married—then you'll get the best of three worlds—Rupert's money—her dowry—and her!

Evelyn Greedy, Major—greedy; No! The lovely Lady Moira is, alas, the one person I would be unable to deceive.

Powell Why?

Evelyn Let us just say—simply—that in certain proportions I am more heroically equipped than Rupert. The shock for poor Lady Moira— agreeable or otherwise—one can only imagine—would nevertheless, alas, reveal me as an imposter. Once Evelyn is dead, I as Rupert will collapse

with remorse and grief—in true theatrical fashion—and promptly post-
pone the marriage. Six months later—I shall cancel it altogether.

Powell She'll sue you for breach of promise.

Evelyn And risk scandal? That family—never! (*He goes to the wardrobe to collect a scarf. His watch is taken off by the Stage Management*)

Powell It's on the cards.

Evelyn Let her try! It must be tonight! (*He looks at his wrist*) That's extraordinary, I could have sworn I just put my watch on ...

Powell I'm so sorry ... (*He produces the watch from his pocket*)

Evelyn Up to your old tricks again, Major!

Powell Force of habit! Is that gold?

Evelyn I went to Aspreys yesterday and charged it to my brother's account. Right then, Major.

Powell You really believe you can pull it off, don't you?

Evelyn Indubitably.

Powell I don't know, sounds too easy. There is one thing you might have overlooked.

Evelyn And that is?

Powell How much is Rupert's life worth. To Rupert. Do you follow me, Mr Farrant. I could visit your brother and inform him of your plan to kill him.

Evelyn Eddie Chan does have a telephone, doesn't he?

Powell Oh ... you wouldn't, would you?

Evelyn And I assure you that I do know the number.

Powell All right. I'll do what you say. I'll kill your brother. I need the money.

Evelyn (*putting on his coat and scarf*) Splendid. On with your hat and coat and off we go.

Powell Where are we going?

Evelyn To Rupert's club. I am going to prove to you that everyone from the hall porter, who will hand me his messages, to the Club Secretary, who will buy us both a very large drink, is going to accept me as Rupert. (*He turns down the bed gas lamp and collects his hat*) Off we go, Major. And for heavens sake, cheer up. What on earth is the matter?

They both move to the front door

Powell What's the matter? I'm worried, that's what's the matter. Very worried indeed. What makes you so bloody sure your precious Rupert will turn up here?

Evelyn That's up to you to persuade him, isn't it Major. If all else fails ... Tell him ... tell him ... I know where the body is buried!!!

Powell You know where the body ... what the hell does that mean?

Evelyn Questions—questions, Major. Relax. Enjoy yourself. You're going to Rupert's club. Leave it all to Rupert Farrant.

Powell (*opening the door*) I'm doing that—with all my fingers crossed.

Evelyn That's the idea. Oh, by the way—have you any money?

Powell Money. What for?

Evelyn A taxi, Major. We can't *walk* to St James's can we?

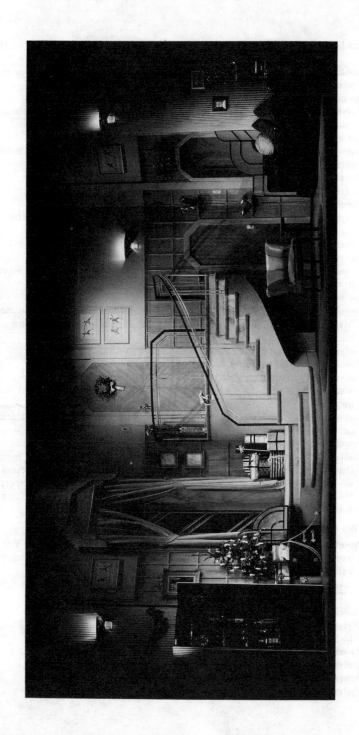

Powell I've a couple of bob.
Evelyn That'll do nicely. Off you go and get a cab.

Powell exits upstairs, past the skylight

Nearly there, Major—nearly there. "Plots have I laid—inductions dangerous, by drunken prophecies, libels and dreams, to set my brother—Rupert—and Major Powell ... in deadly hate ... the one against the other ..." (*He turns the remaining gas lamps off*) Goodnight, Evelyn

Evelyn exits through the front door where his "double" takes over

Powell comes down the stairs

Powell Ah, Mr Farrant ... Mr Farrant, I've got a taxi. He's waiting up on the corner. He wants to know in which direction we're heading.

Powell talks to Evelyn's double then both Powell and the double exit up past the skylight

The real actor playing Evelyn has made a costume change to Rupert and is "discovered" on the balcony of the other set for the "in view" scene change, if a revolve is used

SCENE 2

Rupert's flat. Seven o'clock that night

The flat is elegant and tasteful with a fitted carpet, art deco furniture, pictures on the wall and heavy, expensive curtains. The front door opens on to a small landing which has a walking stick pot on it. A curved staircase leads down from the door, pausing at a lower landing where a pair of french windows R lead out to a small balcony, off. Set inwards from the windows is a set of tasteful heavy curtains, swagged at each side. One curtain can be easily loosened to conceal the exit of actors through the escape. The stairs continue to ground level. A gilt dolphin at the bottom of the banister rail turns on a pivot and is a secret control knob to open double doors hidden in the downstage right pillar. This reveals a huge walk-in drinks cabinet with shelves of glasses and bottles. This should be built so that an actor can be shut up inside, having been impaled against the shelves with a trick sword

Doors up left lead to the bedroom and kitchen. An armchair and small table stand down left. A smart sofa (preferably a three-seater) is fixed against the wall, L, curved to fit in with a pillar. Cushions fill the sofa. A Van Gogh pen-and-ink sketch (small enough to be pocketed) hangs on the wall. At the off-stage end of the sofa is a cupboard containing Rupert's cheque book. A large wireless set sits on top of the cupboard

A sword rack and two epée swords with a goblet and a third spare sword are UL, between the two doors

On the ground level, next to the drinks cupboard, is a small table on which a Christmas tree stands next to a telephone (which has no dial). A stack of

brightly wrapped Christmas presents, set on the middle landing, completes the scene

Rupert is discovered on the balcony of his flat, wearing a dressing gown. He shuts and locks the french windows. Music is playing on the wireless—a piano arrangement of "You Do Something To Me!" There is a knock on the door. Rupert moves upstairs, pausing to straighten a picture at the top of the stairs. He opens the door

Hawkins, a police constable, is on the threshold

Hawkins Good evening, Mr Farrant.
Rupert Hawkins! What can I do for you? Won't you come in?

Rupert descends the stairs

Hawkins Thank you, sir. Hope I am not disturbing you? (*He follows Rupert downstairs*)
Rupert Not at all. Care for a drink? (*He turns the dolphin knob to open the drinks cabinet*)
Hawkins That's very kind, sir.
Rupert Got the evening off?
Hawkins Oh no, sir. The whole force is on standby tonight.
Rupert The King, of course!
Hawkins Yes. As it happens, I'm selling tickets for our Fancy Dress Christmas Buffet and Dance.

Rupert pours a small, not very nice, sherry

Rupert I suppose you want me to buy one.
Hawkins Very good of you, sir.
Rupert I shan't be able to use it.
Hawkins And we've a station raffle tonight too, sir. First prize—two tickets to *Careless Rapture*.
Rupert I've seen that!
Hawkins Second prize—an electric razor. Third prize—one hundred Craven A.
Rupert Oh dear! (*He hands Hawkins the sherry*) I'll get my cheque book. How much? (*He goes to get his cheque book from the cabinet, turning the wireless off*)
Hawkins A shilling a book, and half a crown for the ticket to the dance. I see you got the new Bugatti, sir.
Rupert Arrived this morning.
Hawkins It's a lovely sight. Eight cylinder—twelve point seven litre. Very nice. I've always been mad about cars.
Rupert They only made twenty-five, you know.
Hawkins Wedding present for your young lady, is it?
Rupert Absolutely not! A little reward to myself for services rendered. A pleasing coup on the market in Burmah-Spencer Rubber. I bought in at two-point-five and sold at thirteen. Very satisfactory.
Hawkins You've made rather a killing, sir.
Rupert More of an assassination, wouldn't you say?

Hawkins Could be, sir. (*He sips the vile sherry, reacts to it and puts it down by the tree*) I like your tree. Spending Christmas here, sir?
Rupert No. I'm off to Scotland.
Hawkins In the Bugatti?
Rupert Good God, no—the weather's filthy—there are blizzards in the Highlands. (*He writes the cheque out*) I'm taking the Flying Scotsman overnight from King's Cross. (*He hands the cheque to Hawkins*) There you are, Hawkins.
Hawkins Three shillings and sixpence ... Thank you very much, sir.
Rupert Not at all, I like to do my bit.
Hawkins Well, I'll be on my way. Would you like me to keep an eye on the car, sir. While you're away. (*He begins to go upstairs*)
Rupert Oh I say, thank you Hawkins, that would be splendid. Goodnight to you. Have a good time.
Hawkins Oh, I will, sir. Goodnight to you and a Merry Christmas.

Hawkins exits

The telephone rings

Rupert (*on the phone*) Rupert Farrant. Moira darling ... I was waiting for your call. Yes, of course I am alone, you naughty thing. The servants left midday, I even have to answer the front door myself! Yes ... eleven-fifteen out of King's Cross ... me too ... can't wait ... perhaps we can sneak away to the stables with a blanket or something ... see you tomorrow. Goodnight Moira, sleep well. (*He puts the phone down and is about to go to the bedroom when there is a knock at the front door. He goes and opens the door*)

Powell is at the door

Powell Good evening.
Rupert Good evening.
Powell Is it Mr Rupert Farrant?
Rupert It is.
Powell Powell is the name, sir. Major Powell. I wonder if I could have a word with you?
Rupert What about?
Powell Er ... Could I come in, sir. It's rather serious.
Rupert Really?
Powell It's to do with your brother.

Rupert immediately tries to close the front door on Powell

Please, Mr Farrant, sir, it's desperate.
Rupert It always is. Oh, very well. (*He opens the door wide*)

Powell leaves his coat at the top of the stairs, follows Rupert downstairs and sits in the armchair

Powell Thank you, Mr Farrant, that's most considerate of you ...
Rupert You're out of breath?

Powell I'm not used to walking.
Rupert Have you come far?
Powell St James.
Rupert Why didn't you take a taxi?
Powell I ... couldn't get a cab with the crowds around the Palace. (*He sits in the wing chair*)
Rupert Do sit ... (*he sees that Powell has sat*) ... down. Would you care for a drink?
Powell That's most kind.
Rupert It'll have to be a quick one. I'm going out.

Rupert offers the policeman's untouched sherry to Powell

Powell Whiskey, if you have it. Irish for choice. A small one, though. I live with an ulcer.

Rupert moves back to the cabinet and pours a drink

Rupert They make aggravating companions! (*He offers a tiny whiskey*)
Powell With a splash of water if you don't mind.
Rupert Water

 Rupert exits through the kitchen door

Powell I do hope I haven't called at an inconvenient time? But Evelyn was very insistent.
Rupert (*from the kitchen*) Was he?

Powell looks around the room and steals a silver ashtray. He notices the Van Gogh pen-and-ink sketch. He takes the picture off the wall, turns it over and is about to put it into his jacket pocket

 Rupert enters with the drink which he hands to Powell

Powell Ah! Mr Farrant—you have a superb artistic eye. Love Van Gogh! (*He pronounces it "go"*)

Rupert crosses to the drinks cabinet for his drink

Rupert Van Gogh!
Powell Bless you!
Rupert It's an early pen-and-ink sketch.
Powell Of course. Yes.
Rupert Now ... er ... Mr Powell ...
Powell Major.
Rupert Major. I suppose Evelyn is in some sort of trouble.
Powell Evelyn is dying. (*He sits on the sofa, L*)
Rupert Dying? What of?

Powell indicates "drink" with his hand

 Oh, drink. Major Powell—Evelyn and I haven't seen one another for years.
Powell Is that so?

Rupert The last time I did see him—he was skulking around outside the Zoo across the road—shabbily dressed—looking like a vagrant. I told him—face to face—if he was thinking of coming here I would have him arrested.

Powell He's desperate to see you now.

Rupert I don't believe it.

Powell It's the truth. An old soldier never lies.

Rupert I'm sure he doesn't.

Powell All I am doing, Mr Farrant, is passing on his request to see you. He is dying and he expressed a wish to see you again.

Rupert Well—he's dying at a very awkward time. I'm on my way to Inverness.

Powell He didn't know that. He didn't decide to die just because you're going to Inverness.

Rupert I realize that, Major. Thank you for letting me know. And now I must ask you to leave. I shall be late. (*He moves to the foot of the stairs on the rostrum*)

Powell No. No. You must go to him tonight. Look here ... (*He gets out an envelope with the key inside*) This is his address. The front door key is inside. Let yourself in.

Rupert Why can't he let me in?

Powell He's in bed.

Rupert Dying?

Powell Yes.

Rupert Major—if this is some sort of a trick ...

Powell Why should he want to trick you?

Rupert You obviously don't know my brother. He's the most unmitigated cad God ever put eyes in. If he's ill—why isn't he in hospital?

Powell Can't afford it. Hasn't worked for years.

Rupert Ah—he wants money! I thought so. Is that what you're after? Is that why you are here?

Powell No—no—no—no—

Rupert He won't get a penny out of me. How much has he weasled out of you?

Powell Nothing. Yet.

Rupert Be warned. How long have you known him?

Powell Not very long.

Rupert Well, I think you'd better find out what he's up to. He's no good. Never was any good. Never will be any good. As a child he was always concocting hair-brained schemes. Acting out stupid fantasies. He's mad y'know. Convinced of it. Get to know him a little better and see that I'm right.

Powell Actors are inclined to have a somewhat distorted sense of reality. It's a most unfortunate calling.

Rupert shuts the curtains

Rupert It's a calling for people who don't want to work—and work hard. That was Evelyn all over. Loved to dress up and lounge about in affected poses (*he sits in the wing chair*)—and his mother encouraged him. She found it so amusing— But the real world isn't like that.

Powell No. No. It isn't.

Rupert Pretending to be someone else. Living out of a tiny suitcase. Is that any way for a man to exist. What do you do, Powell? You still in the Army?

Powell Not now. Came out in twenty four.

Rupert What were you in?

Powell Fourth Hussars. Prince Albert's Own. Mons, Ypres. The Somme. It was terrible.

Rupert Are you in business now?

Powell Well ... er ... the truth is I'm more or less retired. But for a while I established an Agency—giving relief to widows and ...

Rupert Samaritan work.

Powell And displaced persons.

Rupert And that is how you met Evelyn?

Powell Oh yes—he was very displaced!

Rupert I don't doubt it. Well, Powell, I've no time for him. Or for people like him. Feckless—selfish—n'er-do-wells with no sense of responsibility. There are far too many of them.

Powell Do forgive me for being presumptuous—but can I offer you a little advice? From someone who is, if I may say, old enough to be your father—You have told me you are a very successful man, sir. And a rich one, if I may be so bold. But money doesn't give you friends. True friends. You will find out who they are, Mr Farrant, when the time comes. And your brother's time has come. You are the only person in the world he has left. If you turn your back on him now—in his hour of need—in later years, it will come to haunt you. Forget your grievances, sir. Obliterate the bitterness of the past. He is your brother, after all. He's an alcoholic. He can't harm you now. Please—take pity. Evelyn— your twin—at this very moment—is lying on his death bed.

Rupert Very eloquent, Powell, but that sort of sentimental guff cuts no ice with me. He's not worth tuppence. And—if you want the truth of it— the news that he's dying is the best Christmas present I'm likely to receive. And now goodnight.

Rupert goes to the cocktail cabinet and leaves his glass. Powell finishes his drink, is about to speak but changes his mind and goes halfway up the stairs, leaving the envelope on the armchair table

Powell There is one other thing, Mr Farrant—

Rupert Yes.

Powell He told me to tell you ...

Rupert What? (*He crosses to the landing and looks up at Powell*)

Powell To tell you ... he knows where the body is buried.

Rupert (*after a long pause*) I'll go and see him *after* dinner.

Powell Splendid. He's dying to see you again. (*He ascends to the front door, collecting his hat and coat*) I'm sure you'll both have a lot to talk about.

Rupert Yes. I'm dreading every minute of it.
Powell You might get a surprise.
Rupert I hardly think so.
Powell What time shall I tell him you'll arrive?
Rupert It's seven now ... in two hours.
Powell About nine o'clock?
Rupert About nine o'clock. And I can't stay long.
Powell Nine o'clock. Couldn't be better. Thank you. Goodnight.
Rupert Goodnight to you.

Powell exits

*Rupert shuts the door after Powell, runs downstairs, then picks up the phone
and speaks to the operator*

(*On the phone*) ... Operator give me Chancery one two seven five please.
This is Regent one two double O. Yes. Thank you. (*He pours his undrunk
sherry back into the bottle*) Oh, Bertram. Good, you haven't left. Something's cropped up I'm afraid. My brother! Yes, apparently he's dying
or something in Soho or somewhere ... I'll have to go to him. I said
nine o'clock but as soon as I've finished packing I've decided to go
straight to him. Could I call by your chambers for a drink? We could
listen to the broadcast together before I take the train ... Oysters! That's
very civil of you. Goodnight Bertram. I'll see you shortly. (*He puts the
receiver down and then crosses to the dolphin which he turns to close the
bar doors. He goes to the armchair and picks up the envelope left by
Powell. He rattles it, then tears it open revealing a key on a tag.*) He
knows where the body is buried! (*He screws up the envelope*)

Rupert exits L

The lights fade to a Black-Out

CURTAIN

SCENE 3

Evelyn's basement flat

*Evelyn is wearing shirt and trousers and trying to get dressed UL. Mrs
McGee is sitting in the armchair with half a bottle of port and a glass, a little tipsy*

Mrs McGee "The moving finger having writ moves on ... a book of verse
a glass of wine and thou, dear Evelyn, singing beside me in the wilder-
ness". Evelyn—may I be so bold as to press you to another small port?

Evelyn crosses to the skip for his shoes

Evelyn Thank you, Mrs McGee—but no. I'm expecting a visitor.
Mrs McGee Oh—you are popular, aren't you? Come here and let me have

a look at you. I've always maintained that men have never mastered the art of dressage. A woman's touch is called for. Allow me to tie your tie.

Evelyn Mrs McGee—please, dear—you must go. This meeting could alter the whole course of my life ... (*He moves to the mirror by the front door to do his bow tie*)

Mrs McGee How exciting! Well—for your sake—I hope your "friend" will be impressed with you. I must say, you dressed like that puts me in mind of Ronald Colman in *Bulldog Drummond.*

Evelyn ... and I don't want you here when he arrives.

Mrs McGee Oh—you don't have to be ashamed of me, Mr Farrant. But may I remind you that this is a respectable house. Though the pantomime that's been going on here lately does give one food for thought you know.

Evelyn What exactly do you mean?

Mrs McGee Far be it for me to expostulate—but the explosions coming from this room this afternoon ...

Evelyn Oh, Mrs McGee—I do most profusely apologize. I was rehearsing a scene out loud from "Pistols at Dawn" and I got a bit carried away! (*He combs his hair and puts his waistcoat on*)

Mrs McGee I understand. You artistes have always had my admiration. (*She gets up and wanders round the room*) I don't know how you do it ... one minute you're up in the clouds—and the next feeling suicidal. I've often remarked to ...

Evelyn ⎫
Mrs McGee ⎭ (*together*) Mrs ... my ... friend at forty three ...

Mrs McGee ... it wouldn't surprise me if I came home to find you in a state of "habeas corpus".

Evelyn And what did she say to that?

Mrs McGee She said she hoped you'd paid the rent first!

Evelyn Well, my dear, if ever you should find me laid out in that dramatic condition—take it all in your stride. Now be a dear—finish your port and pop along to your "friend at forty-three" as you do every Friday.

Mrs McGee To be honest—I just don't fancy tête-à-têtting with her tonight. Besides I've got one of my migraines coming on. (*She sits with her port at the desk*)

Evelyn But ... you can't have ... not tonight!

Mrs McGee Oh, but I have. I should know when I have an incipient migraine. I need to lie down in a darkened room with a cold compress and listen to my King!

Evelyn But you promised to return these napkins. (*He puts the napkins on the desk*)

Mrs McGee She can wait for them. I've rather gone off her. Accusing me of flirting with her husband.

Evelyn Oh, is that what it is! But Mrs McGee surely you know how attractive you are. Undeniably attractive.

Mrs McGee (*preening*) Oh—do you think so Evelyn?

Evelyn Do I have to keep telling you?

Mrs McGee nods her head and giggles

Other women are bound to be jealous. "Oh beware my lady of jealousy, it is the green-eyed monster which doth mock ..." Iago said that.

Mrs McGee Did she? Well, she must be right, I suppose. I never saw it in that light.

Evelyn Well you wouldn't of course. Modesty being one of your finer attributes. But you must go to her tonight—and preen your alluring wiles and you will witness a jealous woman capitulate to your devastating charisma.

Mrs McGee You may have a point there.

Evelyn I certainly do.

Mrs McGee Yes. I suppose I am the sort of personage who is noticed in a crowd. I've weathered rather well.

Evelyn No doubt about that Mrs McGee! (*He moves to open the door for her*)

Mrs McGee That's more than one can say about my friend. No wonder her husband ogles me. Well—perhaps I'll give him something to ogle. (*She moves towards the open front door*)

Evelyn That's the idea.

Mrs McGee Night night ...

Mrs McGee exits with the port bottle, glass and napkins, singing "Has she got saucy eyes ..."

Evelyn Oh God! (*Putting on a voice*) "I'm glad yer don't plan a murder every day, dear—what with her bobbin' in and out!" "Now what's the time". Oh, it's getting on. I must be out of here before he gets here. (*He fetches white gloves from the skip*) "What yer doing now then?" You wait and see: have I got a surprise for you. (*He gets the revolver from the desk*) There. Isn't it lovely? "Oooh, yers. To think a little thing like that can do so much damage. Is it loaded?" Wait. Wait and see ... just you wait and see! (*He cleans the gun with the kitchen towel*) "Oh, I say— yer wipin' all the finger prints off, you are a corker, you are!" I told you ... I think of everything. "Well yer 'ave to, don't you". (*He takes the skull from the shelf on the wall and puts it down next to the gun on the desk*) Now then—where are my three little piggies? "This little piggy went to market ... (*He takes bullets from the skull and loads the gun*) This little piggy went home ... And this little piggy went wee—wee— wee ..." Dead! Careful now! (*He puts the gun in the drawer, nearly dropping it, and returns the skull to the shelf. He turns off the gas lamp DR and returns the gloves to the skip. Crossing to DL he gets "Mother's" photo out of the small drawer, kisses it and sits on the stool hugging it*) My darling mother, I'm doing all this for you. You know that don't you? I promised to kill him. He should not have done it, should he, Mummy? It's wrong to do things like that. He must be punished. He mustn't be allowed to get away with it. And he won't get away with it. He won't ... he won't ... he won't ...

Powell (*off*) Evelyn! Evelyn!

Evelyn No! Too soon! Too soon!

Evelyn rushes to put the photo away, collects his jacket and goes for the door but Powell is coming downstairs outside the flat. Evelyn hides in the cupboard UC

Powell enters and hangs up his hat on the back of the door

Powell Evelyn ... Evelyn ... I'm back, Evelyn. Where the hell is he? Must have a drink. (*He pours from the bottle on the desk*) Bloody actors! Bunch of unreliable, uneducated gypsies! Sitting about in pubs—getting drunk. I ought to know, I almost married one. God! I've got a thirst you can photograph! (*He drinks*) Now. Check the gun. (*He opens the desk drawer to find the gun. This is a second loaded gun, as Evelyn has loaded a replica gun with brass bullets*) Check the gun ... (*He puts it on the desk*) The suicide note ...

Powell searches for the note in the desk but is interrupted by the landlady singing, off

Mrs McGee (*off*) I'm off now Evelyn, see you later. (*Singing*) "Has she got saucy eyes ..."

Powell The landlady ... (*He grabs the towel hanging by the sink and covers the gun on the table*)

The door slams, off

Powell looks out of the window to check she has gone—sags with relief—then returns to the desk, puts the towel back, then looks for the note

The suicide note ...? By the bed. That's it.

Powell searches DS of the bed as Evelyn attempts to move from the cupboard to the front door. He cannot get there and retreats to the cupboard just as Powell turns

Where the hell is it? There's no bloody note! I'll look for it later. (*He moves behind the bed, pulls back the bedspread and prepares the pillows to look like a body in bed. He turns down the gas lamp by bed, and puts the bedspread over the pillows*)

Evelyn's Double attempts to exit from the cupboard but returns inside again. IMPORTANT: the actor playing Evelyn has changed to Rupert and comes downstairs past the skylight windows. Powell rushes to the desk, collects the gun and then hides below the skip in the shadows

Rupert Farrant, wearing a white dinner jacket, enters using the key. He looks around at the flat

Rupert Oh, my God! Hello. (*He comes into the room, pockets the key and closes the front door*) Anyone there? (*He looks at the dishes, then at the broken picture of himself on wall R. He moves above the desk, takes off his glasses and sees the "body" in the bed*) Hello.

Powell takes aim with the gun. Rupert turns. Powell fires. Rupert falls on the bed, then slides off it dragging some bedclothes with him

IMPORTANT: Actor playing Rupert escapes from the set under the bed and changes back to Evelyn, ready to re-enter from inside the cupboard

Powell Oh, my God! What have I done? (*He drops the gun on the bed as he looks at the body behind the bed*) This is terrible. Control yourself, Powell. Control yourself! (*He crosses to the front door*) I feel sick. (*He puts his head in the sink and sees the blinis*) God! The blinkis! (*He crosses to C then sits in the armchair*) Evelyn—where the hell are you? For God's sake—come back. (*He sags into the armchair with his head in his hands*)

Evelyn, in hat, scarf and overcoat, escapes from the cupboard out through the unlocked front door, not seen or heard by Powell

Where the hell is he? (*He stands, moves above the bed and talks to the body that is supposed to be there*) Oh, Rupert ... sorry, Rupert. I needed the money ... Oooh ...

Evelyn is heard rattling the door handle. Powell turns to the front door

The front door opens, Evelyn enters in his hat and coat, wearing "Rupert's" glasses

Powell Evelyn ... Thank God for that!
Evelyn Oh, good evening, Major ... where is my brother?
Powell He's here. Your brother ... Rupert ... he's, oh God ... he's ... I've killed him. Rupert's dead.

Evelyn moves above the desk and takes his hat off

Evelyn Dead? I'm sorry, there must be some mistake. I am Rupert!
Powell You? Rupert? That's impossible ... I ...

Powell backs away from the bed pointing to the body. He moves to the desk. Evelyn crosses to the bed and looks at the body

Evelyn Well—well—well, Major. What have you done?

A small pause

Powell I've shot the wrong bloody brother, that's what I've done! (*He stands, in despair, at the desk*)

CURTAIN

ACT II

SCENE 1

The same. Immediately following

Evelyn, playing "Rupert", is looking at the body behind the bed

As soon as Powell's back is turned Evelyn gets behind the bed and produces something from his pocket. We do not see it. This will be the "blood" setting instrument. He then rifles through the pockets of the body. (Note: There is no need for a "body" to be lying here for this business as the audience cannot see behind the bed) Evelyn can now pick up the wallet. This, of course, is set during the interval by the Stage Management. The dummy gun is also set on the bed and the real one reloaded offstage. Evelyn produces the wallet, which we see. He places it in his own pocket. From his other pocket he produces his own wallet and plants this on "the body". He smiles and slowly comes towards Powell.

REMEMBER: Powell thinks this is Rupert. We know it is Evelyn playing "Rupert".

Evelyn Major—is this some sort of macabre joke? You come to my house—inform me that my brother is dying—and when I get here—he's dead!

Powell He's not supposed to be dead.

Evelyn turns up the bed gas lamp

Evelyn Really. His chest is ripped right open. I've never seen such blood outside an abattoir. If he's not supposed to be dead—what is he supposed to be?

Powell Alive!

Evelyn Alive?

Powell What I'm trying to say is: I didn't do it. Well I did do it—but I wasn't supposed to do it to him. I was supposed to do it—to you! God! I knew it would go wrong!

Evelyn Pull yourself together, man. Calm yourself.

Powell I was merely carrying out my orders. Like an old soldier.

Evelyn What orders?

Powell To kill you! And then your "body" would become his "body" and he would say Evelyn had committed suicide. Oooh—look at him! What a bloody mess! Can't stand the sight of blood.

Evelyn I thought you were a military man?

Powell So I am. Mons. Ypres. The Somme. Terrible.

Evelyn And when my "body" had become his "body"—what then?

Powell I was to put the suicide note he had written beside his body—your body—and then he would become you. (*He finds the folder in the desk*) It's all here—your whole life. You are Rupert, aren't you?

Evelyn How dare you.
Powell (*opening the folder*) What artists do you like?
Evelyn (*quickly remembering*) Artists. Van Gogh. Manet.
Powell Sports?
Evelyn Fencing. Is this a quiz?
Powell Give me the name of your dentist.
Evelyn Patrick McKenzie—twenty-two Cadogan Square. Why? Do you
need a filling?
Powell (*shouting*) I'm not convinced you are Rupert! I'm sorry, Mr Far-
rant—it's just that I'm not sure who anybody is at the moment. As a
matter of fact—I'm not too sure who I am. But, of course you're him.
If you weren't—you wouldn't have turned up as arranged, would you?
Evelyn Obviously.

Evelyn looks around the room to the wig tin. Powell sits on the bed

Powell Of course, he never possessed your suavity—your assurance. He
never had that. What was it you called him—a vagrant. Skulking about
the Zoo. You're right!
Evelyn What was in it for you, Major?
Powell Ten . . . ten thousand pounds!
Evelyn Ten thousand pounds! And where was he going to get that amount
of money from?
Powell Er . . . you! When he had become Rupert Farrant—he would pay
me ten thousand for . . . killing you. You see?
Evelyn When did you and my brother conceive this plan?

Evelyn goes to the desk and reads the folder

Powell This afternoon! He invited me to lunch. We had some awful fish
eggs he kept tossing around in a pan. A few whiskeys, a superb Hock.
I confess it.
Evelyn And over lunch you planned my murder.
Powell Well, I was just listening . . .
Evelyn And the success of this exercise hinged on your setting up a fake
suicide with me as my brother's body?
Powell Yes.
Evelyn With a suicide note, in my brother's hand-writing beside the
corpse?
Powell Yes.
Evelyn Show me the note?
Powell Pardon?
Evelyn Where is it?
Powell I couldn't find it.
Evelyn You're quite sure there was a note?
Powell Oh, yes. He told me there was a note.
Evelyn Then—WHERE IS IT?
Powell You arrived too early—he didn't have a chance to write it—
Evelyn How many suicides have you seen, Major?
Powell Very few, I'm glad to say.

Evelyn In your opinion—I ask merely out of curiosity—is it usual for a suicide to shoot himself in the chest?

Powell I've no idea.

Evelyn I suggest to you that the normal practise is to blow one's brains out!

Powell No—no—he was most insistent on that point. He said he wanted everyone to admire his beauty! "Aim for the heart. If you can find it". That's what he said.

Evelyn You scored a bull's eye, Major!

Powell Well, they always called me "One Shot Wally", you know.

Evelyn I ask you—again—purely out of curiosity—how many of your acquaintances were born with arms ten feet long?

Powell Ten feet long?

Evelyn Any investigating officer with an elementary knowledge of ballistics would determine that the shot that killed my brother was fired at a distance of at least ten feet. A suicide's bullet fired from a gun pressed close against the heart would leave a small—neat—round hole.

Pause. They both look at the body. Powell reacts to the blood

So—what it boils down to is that there is no note! No suicide! And I put it to you that there was no plan to impersonate me either.

Powell But the file I showed you?

Evelyn This file proves nothing beyond the fact that my brother was eaten up with envy of my life style. No, I see the whole thing now ... I was to be the target of a petty swindle cooked up by a pair of shiftless chisellers. You suggested to my brother that you should visit me with some cock and bull story that he was lying on his death bed. Out of charity I could be counted on to cough up some money. But—when you returned and found him drunk and told him I had said I would never part with a penny piece—he grew violent—and in a squalid quarrel—aggravated by drink—you pulled out this gun and murdered him.

Powell No! No!

Evelyn Is there a telephone?

Powell Telephone. No, I don't think so. What for?

Evelyn I'm going to call the police! (*He collects his hat from the desk and crosses to the door*)

Powell Where are you going?

Evelyn I'm going to find somebody in this house and have them summon a constable.

Powell No—Mr Farrant—wait—please—give me a minute—I'm all con-fused—there is another way of looking at this. We're all alone here. The house is empty. I know the landlady's out. No one saw you arrive—or me—so why don't we just do a bunk—and leave him?

Evelyn Do a "bunk"?

Powell Look—didn't you say the best Christmas present you could ever have would be to see your brother dead ...

Evelyn Did I say that?

Powell Yes. Well there he is! Happy Christmas!! Look, Mr Farrant—you don't want to get mixed up with a murder. A man with your position in society. I don't know if you've ever seen a trial at the Old Bailey. Dreadful. They'll call on you—you'll have to give evidence—centre stage—all those wigs! Everyone in black! Even the Judge's hat!

Evelyn A man must do his duty.

Powell But me, Mr Farrant—what about me?

Evelyn You!

Powell Mr Farrant ... I have a confession to make. I am not really a Major—I'm not even a Samaritan. I'm a professional criminal. A despicable, petty criminal. With a long record, I'm afraid. I needed the money, you see. And Evelyn knew it. I'm on the run ...

Evelyn Who from?

Powell Eddie Chan. He's after me all right. I know it.

Evelyn Eddie who?

Powell Eddie Chan. You must have heard of him.

Evelyn (*shaking his head*) No.

Powell He used me as a look-out in twenty-four—when they were unloading crates down in Limehouse.

Evelyn What was in them?

Powell Guns. Raw silk. Opium. All labelled: "Manchurian Water Chestnuts"! I got so nervous I blew the whistle by mistake. They thought the police were coming and ran straight down the East India Dock Road.

Evelyn And Mr Chan wants to kill you for that?

Powell No! ... Well, yes ... I ... er, ... I'm afraid I helped myself to some of the cargo. Then I shot his brother.

Evelyn Shot his brother?

Powell It was a terrible mistake.

Evelyn It must be habit forming.

Powell I thought he was a Customs officer. And then I told a rival gang— the Mazarolli crowd, foreigners, you know—of Chan's future activities.

Evelyn Dear me ... You really are up a monkey tree, aren't you?

Powell Oh, yes ... you have no idea what it's like ... every day ... the fear of being stopped ... bundled into a car ... and then ... garotted ... or worse! Oh, God—I can't run any more ... I'm tired ... I'm old ... I can't live out of suitcases any longer. My life—one long rotten winter. I'll tell them everything ... they'll look after me.

Evelyn Tell who?

Powell The police.

Evelyn The police.

Powell The police, of course. They'll understand. I'll be safe from Chan. I wouldn't be living in fear. I'll be secure. No more running. And in prison I can live a decent enough life. Learn a trade. Become a Samaritan—write my memoirs. You know, the idea is beginning to sound rather attractive.

Evelyn But not practical. It's rather uncomfortable writing your memoirs hanging from the end of a rope!

Powell Oh, God! What am I going to do? Mr Farrant? Who am I to turn to? You're the only one. Please—help me! Please!

Evelyn Listen to me very carefully—and do exactly what I say. It's against every one of my better instincts and contrary to all my principals but I have decided to take pity on you—though God knows I shall probably rue it.

Powell Never—never—I do assure you, my dear sir . . .

Evelyn You are absolutely certain that no one saw me arrive?

Powell Oh, yes—yes—quite certain—quite. The house is deserted. Listen— there's not a sound.

They both listen. Silence

Evelyn Very well. I'm going to leave here now. I shall take this weapon with me. It has your finger-prints on it and would be most potent evidence against you—so don't try any tricks with me. After I've gone—you must tidy this room—remove all evidence of your ever having been here.

Powell What do you mean?

Evelyn You ate a meal here, you say? Your finger-prints will be every- where. On the plates, the silver—the glasses—everything!—Get rid of them all! And—vanish!

Powell Vanish? But—what about the corpse?

Evelyn Put him back in bed. Pull the bedclothes over his wound. Spill the remains of the whiskey on the pillow. If your luck holds—he'll stay there undisturbed right through the weekend. In the event of any one calling— they will think he's in an alcoholic stupor—and leave him to sleep it off. By the time they discover the truth—you'll be in Timbuctoo.

Powell Timbuctoo! I haven't got the fare to Tooting!

Evelyn Come to my house when you've finished here. I'll give you suffi- cient funds to leave the country.

Powell How much?

Evelyn One hundred pounds!

Powell It's not enough!

Evelyn It's all you'll get.

Powell Make it two hundred. Please?

Evelyn All right, Powell—and be as quick as you can.

Powell I will. I will.

Evelyn And take a taxi.

Powell Taxi! I'm skint!

Evelyn Here's five pounds on account.

Powell (*taking the money*) How do I know you won't change your mind and go to the police?

Evelyn You don't. You must live in hope.

Powell I've forgotten your address.

Evelyn (*producing a visiting card from Rupert's wallet*) Here's my card! (*He passes the card to Powell*)

Powell (*taking the card and reading it*) Rupert Farrant. One hundred and Fourteen, Connaught Terrace. You really are Rupert, aren't you?

Evelyn Who did you think I was: my brother, Evelyn?

Evelyn smiles, goes to the front door and exits, taking the gun and the dossier with him

IMPORTANT: The actor must now go and position himself behind the bed to be dragged out as "Rupert"

Powell, alone, in silence, has fear all over his face. He staggers about

Powell Oh, my God! Finger-prints! Everywhere ... yes ... What can I put 'em in? (*He looks round—across to the bed*) Pillow case! (*He runs into the bedroom area—grabs up the pillow case—pulls it off the pillow. Business as he takes pillow to desk then back for pillow case. He empties the goblet in the sink. Goblet goes into the pillow case. Pillowcase to sink, puts in plates and cutlery*) And his brother—can I trust him? Yes. He won't go to the police. He doesn't want to get involved. But suppose he changes his mind? Oh, God, don't think about that now. (*He picks up a blini from the sink*) Bloody blinkies ... (*Picking up the French bread and putting it in the pillow case, he looks at the body*) Heroically equipped! (*The large chopping board goes into the full pillow case. He crosses to the whiskey bottle on the table by the armchair*) Fingerprints! (*Business as he cleans bottle with cloth and manages to put more prints on with other hand! Leaves bottle on desk. Crosses to above bed*) And I've got a corpse on my hands! A dead one!

Powell lifts the head of the body up and puts it down. This is the real Rupert wearing a bloodstained white dinner jacket. The stains must not be seen by the audience

Oh, God I forgot the lights ... (*He turns off the bed lamp, then turns down the centre lamp. Pulls bedspread off the bed, and covers the body. He lifts the body upright, staggers about and drops him over the back of the armchair*) Don't go away ... I'll be back! (*He tidies the bed, and returns to lift the body up*) I'm back! ... One, two, three ...

As he lifts the body upright Mrs McGee is heard singing, off

Mrs McGee (*off*) "Has she got saucy eyes ..." Evelyn—is that you in there, dear?

The body starts to fall forward but Powell pulls it back and leans it against the cupboard doors, putting a wreath from a hook over doors on its head. Evelyn appears to be wearing another costume!

(*Off*) It's me, dear Evelyn ... Let me in dear, I know you're in there, because I can hear you ... I'm coming in ... I'm getting my key out ... I'm putting it in the lock ...

Mrs McGee staggers in tipsier, but delightfully so

And here I am! "Has she got saucy eyes ... yes she has ..." I've never been so insulted in my life ... My friend threw me out! Hello Evelyn ...

Powell is hiding behind the body and waves Evelyn's left arm at her

I said "hello" Evelyn ...
Powell Hello ...
Mrs McGee Oh, and what part are you playing now dear?

Powell (*mumbling*) Mmmmmm ho ho ho ...
Mrs McGee Oh, the Spirit of Christmas Yet to Come!

The body slowly starts to topple forward but is pulled back by Powell just in time

Oh, Evelyn, our moment is upon us ... if you want me ... woo me! (*She turns to face the body*) What's the matter? Are you lost for words?
Powell Go away! (*He waves Evelyn's arm about*)
Mrs McGee Well, if that's the way you're going to behave, I want what's due to me at once. Three pounds, fourteen shillings and eleven pence halfpenny. That includes three and five pence for the milk and meter. Now let me have it.

Powell circles Rupert's arm about. Mrs McGee tries to grab it

Stop waving at me! And give me my money. It's so dark in here I'll turn the gas lamp up ...
Powell Mrs McGee ... (*He reaches in his own trouser and brings out the five pounds Evelyn gave him*)
Mrs McGee (*romantically*) Yes ... Oh, thank you, dear. (*She takes the money and counts it, hand to hand*) One ... two ... three ... four ... FIVE.

Powell snatches back the fifth note

Well, I'll keep the change! Oh, Evelyn ... Won't you come upstairs with me ... it's so much cosier there ...

Powell lifts Rupert's arm so that hand falls over Rupert's face

Oh ... You're not quite up to it! Well, *c'est la vie!*

Mrs McGee exits

(*As she goes*) "Has she got saucy eyes ..."

Powell waves Rupert's arm "goodbye". The moment Mrs McGee has gone Powell staggers with the body to the bed. They both fall on to the bed and Evelyn slides off upstage leaving Powell struggling to stand upright. IMPOR-TANT: Actor playing Rupert escapes under the bed and double takes his place

Powell I'll never be the same again!

Powell stands and moves behind the bed. He pulls the body's head onto the bed and tries to lift his feet, but gives up and lets the foot fall on his own toes. He limps

Oh, to hell with it! (*He collects the pillow case*) Wait, wait ...! The whiskey. (*He pours whiskey over the body, putting down the pillow case to do so*)

Got to get away! Leave the country. Tonight!

Powell goes to exit, then remembers the pillow case and returns to collect it

Bloody blinkies!

Powell exits up the fire escape stairs

There is a pause. The body slowly raises his arm, stretches, groans and sits up on the bed, facing up stage. He then falls forwards to the bed with his head in his hands

The lights fade to a Black-out

CURTAIN

SCENE 2

Rupert's flat

Darkness. Evelyn enters with the Rupert file. He is wearing his hat and gloves

Evelyn I've done it. (*He switches on the lights*) Oh, my God! My poor child, such a place. Here's a fine kettle of fish indeed. I see the maid has certainly been in here today. (*He comes downstairs*) Poor Rupert! (*He places the dossier on the ledge by the telephone*) But I'm not sorry for him. (*He produces some wirecutters and puts them on the sofa. Then he begins whistling "You Do Something to Me!". Looking into the bedroom*) Bedroom ... (*He opens the kitchen door and leaves it open*) Kitchen ... (*He looks at his watch, turns on the wireless and checks his gun, which he leaves on the table by the armchair*)

But soft! About your grisly business ...
Go, go—dispatch ... (*He leaves the gun on the armchair table*)

The King's Abdication speech is heard on the wireless

Edward (*on the wireless*) ... and to discharge my duties as King, as I would wish to do, without the help and support of the woman I love ...
Evelyn "God save King George, unkinged Edward says ..."
Edward (*on the wireless*) And I want you to know that the decision I have made ...

The phone rings. Evelyn turns off the wireless set

Evelyn Rupert Farrant ... who? Ah, Bertram! Oh, I'm sorry, I got held up. No nothing serious, he was going to commit suicide. I talked him out of it. He was depressed ... Everything's fine. ... Yes, I was listening to it here. ... "He did all this and could not get a crown". *Henry VI* Part three Act three Scene two ... Shakespeare Bertram!, I'll give your love to Moira. Yes. And a very Happy New Year to you! (*He puts the phone down and looks around the room*) "Would you like a drink Evelyn?" Oh, my God yes, Rupert, I most certainly would! But where does he keep his drink?

There is a knock at the door. Evelyn goes to answer it

Come in.

Powell enters, nervously and quickly, and goes downstairs

Evelyn closes the door

Powell I've cleaned everything up!

Evelyn Really?

Powell I'm sure of it. I'm a dab hand at that sort of thing. Not a trace of me left in that room. I shoved everything into a dirty pillow case.

Evelyn Where is it now?

Powell At the bottom of the Boating Lake. I took a taxi to the park, stopped on the bridge and chucked the whole lot over, including my hat and coat.

Evelyn What!

Powell I told the cabbie I'd broken a mirror and was dropping the pieces in running water.

Evelyn Dropping the pieces in running water?

Powell That stops the seven years bad luck.

Evelyn I didn't know that.

Powell Ah, well, you're not Irish.

Evelyn What did the cabbie say?

Powell Thank God he was from County Mayo!

Evelyn You're sure it sank?

Powell It's weighed down with nigh on half a bloody ton of old paving stone. Almost pulled my arm out of the socket heaving it over the parapet and I paid off the taxi and then walked the rest of the way here.

Evelyn What did you do with the body?

Powell Tucked him up in bed. He'll sleep there till Domesday. Where's the money and I'll be on my way.

Evelyn I've been thinking the whole thing over, Powell. I've already given you five pounds—

Powell I had to give four of that away to the landlady. She called for the rent. Had a very tricky moment with her, let me tell you.

Evelyn What happened?

Powell Don't ask!

Evelyn She didn't come into the room?

Powell She did. It's all right. She didn't notice a thing. She was soused and I was too fly! But she nicked four quid for the rent. Then the taxi cost almost two bob. So, once again yours truly is skint. I'd like it in cash!

Evelyn I'm not giving you another penny.

Powell What!

Evelyn I'm not giving you any money. I've thought it over—I've behaved like an idiot. I should have called the police as soon as I found my brother's body.

Powell Are you having me on?

Evelyn I'm deadly serious. I can't afford to be mixed up in a scandal, withholding evidence.

Powell I warn you, Mr Farrant, I'm a desperate man. I've killed once today—so I've got nothing to lose. Aaaaah! (*He falls into the armchair*)

Evelyn What's the matter?

Powell My stomach! The ulcer. Oooh—my tablets!

Evelyn Get up—and get out!
Powell Give me some water.

Evelyn moves to the kitchen door.

Evelyn Water.

As soon as Evelyn's back is turned Powell grabs the gun from the table and stands up

Powell Mr Farrant!

Evelyn turns

Evelyn Don't be a fool.
Powell I'm no fool. I want my money—you'd better give it me.
Evelyn I'm not afraid of you. I've never been afraid of anyone. I'm going to call the police. Give me that gun! (*He moves towards Powell*)
Powell Stay away! Or I'll fire ...

They struggle with the gun, gradually moving off stage to the kitchen. Pots and pans are heard crashing about as they continue to struggle. A shot is fired

Evelyn enters and clutches the back of the sofa

Evelyn Powell ... Powell ...

Evelyn falls behind the sofa, out of view, with his left arm extended in full view of the audience. IMPORTANT: this is a false arm. Actor playing "Evelyn" now goes to Rupert's front door to enter as "Rupert", in white dinner jacket

Powell enters, very shaken

Powell There's another one! I've killed another one!

The phone rings

There's no one here.

The phone rings

They're all dead.

The phone rings

Please stop ...

The telephone stops ringing as Powell points the gun at it

My God! Thank you. The file! (*He grabs it*) I've got to get out of here ... get down to Dover ... take the boat train to ... (*He tears up the stairs to the front door, and opens it*)

We see Rupert Farrant standing on the threshold, covered in blood

Powell, on seeing him, shrieks, and immediately slams the front door in fright

AH! My God! Another one! How many more are there?

There is a loud banging on the front door

Rupert (*off*) Open this bloody door!!

Powell opens the door

Rupert stands there. He enters and slams the door behind him. We know it is the real Rupert. Powell thinks it is Evelyn

What the devil are you doing here?

Powell Please ... Evelyn ...

Rupert I'm not bloody Evelyn ... I'm Rupert! (*He staggers down the stairs*)

Powell Ah—you can't pull that trick on me. I know your game. You promised me ten thousand if I killed him. Well, you can impersonate him now. Just give me my money.

Rupert Ten thousand ...

Powell Don't pretend you don't know what I'm talking about. You came too early, you fool. I shot you—thinking it was him.

Rupert shakes his head in total disbelief

Rupert Now, look here, Major.

Powell No—he wouldn't believe me either. I had to show him your file. There it is!

Rupert This is absolutely incredible. (*He frantically looks through the file*)

Powell Isn't it! The whole thing is incredible. It's incredible that you're standing here .... it's incred ... as a matter of fact—how is it you are here?

Rupert You ask me that? I wake up in Soho, in one of the grimiest hovels I've ever seen—stinking of whiskey and sodden with blood—which turns out not to be blood at all—no wound that I can find—merely a very nasty headache. My pocket picked—save for one note—in my brother's unmistakable scrawl. (*He takes out the note and gives it to Powell*)

Powell (*reading*) "Dearest Brother, go to your house immediately. I shall be there—waiting—waste no time, I beg you! Evelyn"

Rupert What the bloody hell is going on Major?

Powell I don't know. Ask him!

Rupert Where is he?

Powell There! (*He indicates the body behind the sofa*)

Rupert My God! (*He crosses to the body*)

Powell Shot! During a struggle.

Rupert A struggle with whom?

Powell With me. He was coming towards me—

Rupert You incompetent Army twit—put a gun in your hand and you fire at anything that moves! You killed him. You've killed Evelyn!

Powell You are Evelyn! I've killed Rupert. You owe me ten thousand pounds!

Rupert I owe you nothing. *He* was going to pay *you* ten thousand pounds to bump me off?

Powell Yes. No! *You* are going to pay *me* ten thousand for bumping *him* off!

Rupert moves to the phone

What are you doing?

Rupert What do you think? The police!

Powell Put down that phone. (*He produces the gun*) Move away!

As Rupert moves away from the phone Powell rips the phone cord from its socket

Rupert Look—listen to me—there isn't any money here. I was on my way to Scotland. A cheque—will you take a cheque?

Powell A cheque! Don't be so bloody stupid. You think you're clever, don't you! Muddling me with your disguises. You're not as clever as you think.

Rupert I'm a man with influence. I'll make sure you won't hang for killing him. I am Rupert Farrant ... I'm very well connected ...

Powell You are Evelyn Farrant, and you still owe me two bob for the taxi! (*He aims the gun at Rupert*)

Rupert Believe me, I can prove who I am ... my wallet ... (*Realizing he does not have his wallet*) My God! (*He runs to the stairs*)

Powell Get down from there! You won't get out that way.

Rupert realizes the only way out is by the balcony. As discreetly as possible he edges towards the curtains

Rupert Believe me—I am who I say I am. Look ... What do you want? The Van Gogh you liked so much ... I'll give it to you ...

Powell Van Gogh ... I hate art ... and artists ... Actors ... degenerates ... bohemians ... and they're always trying to cadge a free meal ...

Rupert is now at the curtain. He decides to make a dash—shouting "help"—as he opens the curtains.

Stay where you are, or I'll fire.

Powell fires at the body going through the curtain. Then a hand is seen through the split of the curtains—it frantically clutches one side of the curtain and falls to the floor, pulling the curtain down. Powell, horrified, staggers back. IMPORTANT: This is the substitute, wearing an identical blood-stained jacket, who is placed off-stage behind the curtains ready to fall as soon as Rupert falls through them

The actor playing Rupert, having disappeared from our view through the curtains, should leave the balcony area and take up his position behind the sofa ready to emerge as "Evelyn"

(*Stunned*) There's another one! I've shot another one! This morning I hadn't heard of Evelyn and Rupert Farrant. Now I've killed them, both! Twice! I can't cope with this any longer. I've got to get out of this madhouse before I kill someone else! You never know—there might be triplets! He must have a bit of cash somewhere! ... the drawer ... I'll try the drawer ... (*He crosses to the phone table, pulls open the top drawer and rifles through it*)

As Powell does this a hand appears over the top of the sofa—this is Evelyn.
He drags himself into our view. He is immaculate in black overcoat and
glasses

Evelyn If you find the whiskey, Major, do pour one out for me!

Powell (*turning*) Thank you! (*He turns back, double-takes*) Aaaah! My
God!

Evelyn Almost fell asleep down there... got the most awful pins and
needles! Well done, Major, I was beginning to wonder how long it
was going to take you. But "One Shot Wally" always gets his man!

Powell Evelyn ...

Evelyn That's right, dear.

Powell Then he's ...?

Evelyn Right again. Major Powell. This time you've really killed him! No
fake blood now!

Powell Fake blood?

Evelyn "Kensington Gore" we call it in the theatre. Amazing stuff! Just
like the real thing, wouldn't you say?

Evelyn takes out the small squirter and squirts a little in Powell's hand.
Powell shows his hand—covered in "blood"

Alas! There's very little left. I've used so much today.

Evelyn crosses to the sofa and takes his coat off

Powell (*firing the gun at Evelyn which just clicks*) You bastard!

Evelyn It's pointless to fire that gun at me—there aren't any bullets in it.
Not even a blank! (*He goes to the body wrapped in the curtain to check
for no pulse*) One little piggy went to market—covered in curare (*he
indicates Rupert*). A blank little piggy stayed home (*he indicates himself*).
And this little piggy went weee—weee—wee—dead! Three shots. A
poisoned dart. A blank. And the real McCoy!

Powell Curare! You mean when I shot him in Soho—

Evelyn Bravo, Major! A poison dart tipped with curare. Along the Ama-
zon the Indians trap their prey that way. But of course, this was not a
fatal whack. Merely a few grains sufficient to render him unconscious.
Is anything the matter, Major?

Powell I ... I ... I'm feeling dizzy ...

Evelyn Do you believe in fate, Major Powell? (*He gets out the front door
keys*)

Powell Fate! No, I don't believe in fate. Codswallop! Look—Mr Farrant—just give me some money and let me scarper.

Evelyn Please I want to tell you about my objectives—(*He goes upstairs
and locks the front door*)

Powell Mr Farrant—all I want to do is get out of here ...

Evelyn My objectives—

Powell Yes, yes, of course, your objectives ...

Evelyn There were three of them. (*He descends the stairs*) First objective
Rupert had to die. That troubled me not a whit! You believed me this

afternoon didn't you when I told you I wanted to be him. It was a lie.
I loathed him and everything he stood for.
Powell But what about the file, and all that stuff about him, what you said
at lunch. Do you mean that was just a game?
Evelyn Well done Major—that foetid brain begins to stir. You have been
bamboozled Powell! No, all I wanted was his money. Second objective,
so that I could become the great actor manager that is my destiny. He
had to die, but not by my hand, though. I had to be there when it
happened.
Powell But I could have done it this evening with a proper bullet.
Evelyn The murder had to take place here.
Powell Then what in God's name did you get him to Soho for?
Evelyn Patience, Major. You'll aggravate your ulcer!
Powell Fat lot you care about my rotten ulcer! You're cruel, you are—
you're as bad as 'im! I'm an old man. I'm sick. Haven't been well lately.
Evelyn You haven't far to go now, Major.
Powell And what in God's name does that mean? If it had to be here, why
didn't you just send me here with the gun this evening. I could have
done it easy as pie!
Evelyn No, no, I had to be there when it happened. He would never have
allowed me across the threshold. I had to lure him to Soho—knock him
out—take his house keys and his wallet—slip a cryptic note into his
pocket—come here—and wait for you and him to follow.
Powell But why did you get me into all this!
Evelyn I needed an executioner.
Powell But why did you choose me?
Evelyn You were the only possible candidate, Major, with your very particular qualifications!
Powell Well what was your third objective?
Evelyn I'll come to that in one moment.
Powell You don't know what you've been putting me through with your
games! First he's dead—then he isn't—then he is—and if it isn't him—
it's you! One minute you're dead and the next you're popping up again
like a bloody jack-in-the box! Why are you wearing gloves?

Evelyn takes his jacket off

Evelyn Yes—it's been a bad day for you, hasn't it? (*He moves the table
from beside the armchair to DL, out of the way*) You've really suffered
all day long. I've watched you ... It was very agreeable. Wire cutters.
Powell You're mad ...
Evelyn Mad? "Who sir? Not I sir! I am as well in my wits, fool, as thou
art". (*He moves the armchair to under the stairwell. He takes the wire
cutters and uses them to free the two swords in the rack*)
Powell What ... are you doing now?
Evelyn "Give them the foils, young Osric. Cousin Hamlet you know the
      wager ...?"
      "... Very well, my my lord; Your Grace hath laid the odds o' the
      weaker side ..."

"... "Then, venom, to thy work ...,""

(*He throws a sword to Powell*)

Powell Please—I have not done this for years ...
Evelyn Think'st thou I am an executioner.

Attack and parry. Powell is disarmed. Powell staggers back to the closed cocktail cabinet

Powell But why? What have I done?
Evelyn Major Ambrose Walter Powell. Real name Murphy. Other pseudonyms: Saunders Newman, Butterworth. We'll skip your early life—one year as shoddy as the next. The important date is eighteen-ninety-eight. You're twenty-three years old, you run away to Canada. With a beautiful girl ...
Powell Kitty Lawrence.
Evelyn Kitty Lawrence. Actress. She was beautiful. She was talented.
Powell Please ... no ...

Evelyn kicks the fallen sword through the air to Powell. Powell catches it

Evelyn "My Father, methinks I see my Father".
Powell God! You ... no ...
Evelyn She was alone—and you left her—outside Farrants Lodging House, Red Deer, Alberta. Hardly an auspicious place for me to make an entrance, Mr Murphy. That is why we were named Farrant. I told Rupert, one day I'd find out where the body was buried.
Powell WHOSE BODY?
Evelyn Your body, Mr Murphy. "Daddy's dead. Daddy's dead and buried". That's what Rupert said. "He's not dead", I said and even if he *is* dead, one day I'll find out where the body is buried and now I've dug it up. Such a pity I can't tell Rupert. Hello, Daddy!!

Powell looks at the windows—a possible way to escape. Evelyn jumps in front of them

Powell Look son ... it's been so long ... I was very young ... irresponsible ... Wrong of me I know ... unforgivable ...
Evelyn I get it from her, you know. My talent.
Powell Yes. Yes. I can see that.
Evelyn Nothing from you. Nothing!
Powell Of course not. I'm not artistic. Look, you're very clever. I think I can help you. I have a friend who is an agent ...

Poewell attacks Evelyn. Their parries fall against the dolphin. The bar opens

Evelyn Oh—that's where he keeps the drinks!

Powell is disarmed again

  Pick it up. Pick it up!
Powell Who do you think you are—Douglas Bloody Fairbanks!?

Evelyn slashes Powell across the rear

Ahhh!

Evelyn "A hit, a very palpable hit!"

Powell You're going to kill me, is that it? By slashing me to death . . .?

Four strokes and Evelyn disarms Powell again

Evelyn Death arrives in a variety of disguises.

Powell And then what?

Evelyn Let myself out quietly. Return home. In an hour's time I shall call Baker Street police station. "Is that the police? I saw something 'orrible outside Connaught Terrace. Figures fighting against the window. And there was a bang!" When the police arrive they'll find my brother shot by a gun that bears your finger prints, and your heart pierced by a sword that bears his.

Powell What about your finger prints eh? Forgotten that hadn't you! (*He runs halfway up the stairs*)

Evelyn Gloves Major. Catch! (*He throws the sword backwards to Powell*)

Powell (*catching the sword*) They might trace me to your place.

Evelyn I thought all the evidence is lying at the bottom of the boating lake. Isn't that what you did! Isn't that what you did?

Powell Damn you! Damn you! Go on—kill me then! You killed your brother!

They fight up the stairs. Powell drops his sword down the stairs. Evelyn is behind Powell holding the blade on the sword across Powell's throat

Evelyn You killed my brother.

Powell And I suppose I killed your mother.

Evelyn You did.

Powell And now you're going to kill your father! God the whole family is on the verge of extinction!

Powell elbows Evelyn in the stomach and escapes downstairs. Evelyn follows by jumping over the stair rail

You're my son, all right. We're both failures, hiding behind our disguises.

Sword fight. Evelyn allows Powell to push him off stage into the kitchen. Powell slams and locks the door throwing the key away. IMPORTANT: Evelyn swaps real sword for trick one.

Ha, ha! And I'll tell you something else for nothing, she was not the goddess you thought she was . . .

Evelyn enters from the bedroom. Powell double-takes

Evelyn She was pure!

Powell She was dull—she was boring—and she was a bad actress!

They fight, progressing nearer to the open bar doors

Evelyn Never! Never! DEATH!!!

Powell No! No! Evelyn . . . Rupert . . . Oh God . . .

Powell lunges, Evelyn disarms him

Evelyn Third objective! "Death for a deadly deed!"

Evelyn impales Powell through the heart inside the bar
  "Down—down to hell—and say I sent thee hither!"

Powell's body slumps up against the shelves
  "Now God and your arms be prais'd, the day is ours, the bloody dog is
  dead!" I'm so tired. Did I do it right, Mummy? I promised you I'd kill
  him. Did I do it right? Oh, Major Powell. You fool. You fool. You
  caused all this. Not Rupert. (*He crosses to the dead Rupert and lifts the
  body's hand up*) "Though I did wish him dead—I hate the murderer—
  love him murdered . . ."

*There is a knock at the door. Evelyn freezes. Second knock at the door.
Evelyn looks around wildly*

Hawkins *(off)* Mr Farrant! Mr Farrant! Can I have a word with you?

The knocking continues
  Mr Farrant!

Evelyn (*to himself*) I'll have to answer. (*Calling*) Who is it?

Hawkins (*off*) Hawkins.

Evelyn Hawkins?

Hawkins (*off*) It's Hawkins, Mr Farrant.

Evelyn One moment . . .

*Evelyn tidies the room—turns the dolphin to shut Powell inside the bar,
returns Powell's sword to the rack, hides the gun under a cushion on the sofa,
collects the door keys from his jacket and drags "Rupert's" body out of the
way into window recess*

Hawkins (*off*) Mr Farrant.

Evelyn Just coming. (*He covers the body with a curtain and Christmas
  presents and swags the remaining curtain up out of the way*)

Hawkins (*off*) Mr Farrant!

*Evelyn rushes upstairs turning out the main lights and taking off his gloves.
The room is now lit by the Christmas tree lights and moonlight through the
open curtains. Snow falls outside. Evelyn opens the door carefully*

Evelyn I'm so sorry—I was on my way to bed . . .

To Evelyn's surprise he learns that Hawkins is a police constable in uniform

Hawkins To bed, sir? Not going to Scotland?

Evelyn No, I'm going in the morning. What do you want?

Hawkins It's your lights, sir. You've left them on.

Evelyn Lights?

Hawkins On the car.

Evelyn On the car? Oh—yes—the car—my car—yes—thank you, constable. I'll slip down in a moment and turn them off. (*He tries to shut
  the door*)

Hawkins Are you all right, sir?

Evelyn Of course I'm all right. Why shouldn't I be all right?

Hawkins Can I come in a moment, sir.

Evelyn It's very late.

Hawkins It is serious.

Evelyn reluctantly opens the door and Hawkins enters, carrying some cigarettes under his cape. Evelyn closes the door

Evelyn Oh, very well.

Hawkins Thank you, sir.

Evelyn What is it?

Hawkins Well, sir, your Bugatti's in a terrible state, sir. It's mounted the kerb—parked half-way across the pavement and the off-side fender's smashed. You can't leave it like that, sir.

Evelyn No ... I ...

Hawkins And to tell you the truth—you practically ran me down half-an-hour ago in the Marylebone Road. I was on my way here with your prize. You've won a hundred Craven A. (*He produces the cigarettes*)

Evelyn Oh, put it with the other Christmas presents, constable.

Hawkins I tried to phone you earlier to tell you about it but there was no answer. To be honest with you, Mr Farrant, I should by rights book you—driving crazy like that—but, well, as it's Christmas ... So, if you just give me the keys I'll go down and see if I can shift it!

Evelyn I think I must have left the keys in the car, constable. Let's get out of this house, then we'll search for them together ...

Hawkins You'd better put a coat on, sir—you'll catch your death!

Evelyn Yes—yes of course ... (*He goes to the sofa to get his coat*)

Hawkins looks around the room

Hawkins I think perhaps you ought to call the all-night garage in Baker Street, sir. Shall I do it? (*He tries the phone but it is dead*) That's funny. (*He picks up the broken cable*) Can you explain, sir?

Evelyn   I can add colours to the chameleon,
                       Change shapes with Proteus for advantages,
                       And set the murd'rous Machiavelli to school.
                       Can I do this, and cannot get a crown ...?
                       Tut! Were it further off—I'd pluck it down

(*He takes his overcoat, then doubles up with maniacal laughter*)

Hawkins What? (*He joins in the laughter*)

Evelyn Come along, constable, and I'll give you a hand with the car.

Hawkins You're not yourself tonight are you, sir?

Evelyn No, you're absolutely right, it's been a very confusing day. I'm so glad it's all over. Well, come along constable, let's go down and shift that car ...

Evelyn puts his coat on. As he goes upstairs he knocks the dolphin with his sleeve. The bar doors open and Powell's body falls out, with the sword still sticking out of him. Hawkins turns, rushes down to the body, then looks up at Evelyn. Evelyn clicks his fingers in exasperation

Evelyn Would you care for a drink, constable?

There is a Black-out

CURTAIN

FURNITURE AND PROPERTY PLOT

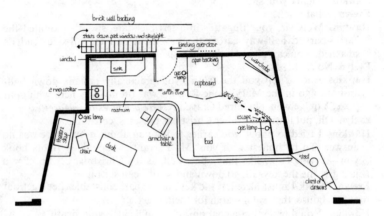

EVELYN'S FLAT

On stage: KITCHEN AREA

Practical two-ring gas stove
Sink with practical taps
Two frying pans on wall.
Other "dressing" pans on wall.
Picture of Rupert prepared to be smashed (sugar glass)
Small chopping board and knife in front of stove
Box of matches
Onions in basin on shelf above stove
Towel on hook DS of stove
Cutlery box. *In it:* knives, forks, two spoons and spare chopping knife
Other dressing around stove includes spare spatula
Two plates in cupboard under stove
Spare wine bottle half corked in cupboard under sink
Oil jug, salt jar, pepper pot, batter jug on shelf to R of stove
Wooden spatula
Mirror on shelf above sink taps
Soap and saucer R of mirror
Sour cream jug and spoon R of soap
Two wine glasses

Two goblets
Corkscrew
Other dressing as desired

BEDROOM AREA
Bed. *On it:* faded counterpane, sheets, two cushions, two pillows in
pillow cases, bolster, open and empty hatbox, newspaper folded in
half
Curtained recess
Wardrobe
Large cupboard. *On it:* Christmas wreath

LIVING AREA
Desk. *On it:* big chopped board, large knife, small knife, watch. *Under
it:* wastebin. In drawer: folder, dummy gun, unloaded
Upright chair
Armchair
Small table
Skull on shelf
Theatre skip. *In it:* theatrical clothes, including white gloves
Gold stool
Chest of drawers. *On it:* wig tin. *In it:* cold cream, mother's photo

ACT I

SCENE 1

Off stage: Napkins (Mrs McGee)

Revolver **(Evelyn)**

Personal: **Evelyn** (as "Queen Mary"): Under coat: wine bottle, corked on harness,
whiskey bottle on harness. In pocket of coat: pot of pâté, pot of caviare,
In left leg garter: Gentleman's Relish. Ellen Terry beads, ear rings,
gloves, handbag. Umbrella containing French loaf
Powell: gold watch on fob chain, two shillings in silver, gold wrist-watch
(double of Evelyn's for pick-pocket business)
Mrs McGee: handbag, bunch of pass keys

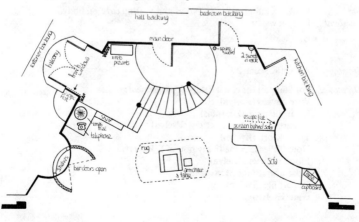

RUPERT'S FLAT

On stage: On main landing: pot with walking sticks
             On middle landing: curtains at window, pile of Christmas presents, dol-
                phin on banister rail
             In main area:
             Christmas tree (with practical lights)
             Telephone (with no dial)
             Shelf beside Christmas tree
             In bar: two whiskey tumblers, two sherry glasses, sherry bottle, whiskey
                bottle. All other bottles and glasses are dressing
             Armchair
             Table
             Sofa with a screen behind
             Cupboard. *On it:* wireless silver ashtray. *In it:* cheque book and pen
             Pictures on wall, including Van Gogh pen and ink drawing
             Two swords in a rack, spare sword below stairs
             Silver cup above swords

SCENE 2

Off stage: Jug of water (**Rupert**)

Personal: **Rupert:** glasses
              Powell: envelope, pills

SCENE 3

On stage: As Scene 1

Off stage: Port bottle and glass (**Mrs McGee**)

ACT II

SCENE 1

On stage: As Act 1, Scene 3

Set: Wallet containing five £1 Notes and visiting card on body
Personal: **Evelyn:** wallet

SCENE 2

On stage: As Act I, Scene 2

Off stage: Pot and pan for crash (**Stage Management**)
              Wire cutters (**Evelyn**)
              Cigarette prize (**Hawkins**)
              Rupert's keys on leather tag (**Evelyn**)
              Trick sword (**Evelyn**)
              Note ("Please come to my house") (**Rupert**)
              Blood squirter (**Evelyn**)
              False arm (**Stage Management**)
              Rupert file (**Evelyn**)
              Gun (**Evelyn**)

Personal: **Powell:** handkerchief
            Evelyn: coat, hat, gloves, watch

GUNS: Two guns are used. A dummy replica for Evelyn to load with brass dummy bullets and one real revolver (5 shot .38 Smith and Wesson Revolver "Chief Special") to fire blanks, loaded and checked by Stage Manager

Suggested setting when a revolve is not available

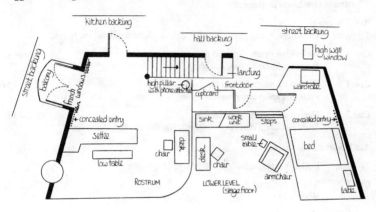

LIGHTING PLOT

Two interior settings. Practical fittings required: three gas lamps in Evelyn's flat. Christmas tree lights in Rupert's flat

Act I, Scene 1

To open: Darkness, except for light through skylight windows on to bed

Cue 1 As Evelyn opens door to flat (Page 2)
Bring up lights to full, gas lamps on

Cue 2 Evelyn turns down gas lamp by bed (Page 15)
Fade gas lamp and covering spot

Cue 3 Evelyn turns off other lamps (Page 17)
Fade gas lamp and covering spot, leaving skylight back light

Act I, Scene 2

To open: Full lighting, including Christmas tree lights

Cue 4 At end of Scene 2 (Page 23)
Black-out

Act I, Scene 3

To open: All practicals on with covering spots

Cue 5 Evelyn turns down gas lamp DR (Page 25)
Fade gas lamp and covering spot

Cue 6 Powell turns down gas lamp by bed (Page 26)
Fade gas lamp and covering spot

Act II, Scene 1

To open: Same lighting as at end of Act 1, Scene 3

Cue 7 Evelyn turns up gas lamp by bed (Page 28)
Bring up gas lamp and covering spot

Cue 8 Powell turns off gas lamp by bed, and centre lamp (Page 33)
Fade gas lamp and covering spots

Cue 9 As body falls forward (Page 35)
Black-out

Act II, Scene 2

To open: Darkness

Cue 10 Evelyn switches on lights (Page 35)
All lights on including Christmas tree

Cue 11 Evelyn turns out lights (Page 44)
All lights off except Christmas tree. Moonlight shows through window

EFFECTS PLOT

ACT I

Cue 1	As Curtain rises *Street noises. Fade as Evelyn enters flat*	(Page 1)
Cue 2	As Scene 2 begins *Piano music from radio*	(Page 17)
Cue 3	Rupert switches radio off *Cut music*	(Page 18)
Cue 4	Hawkins exits *Telephone rings*	(Page 19)

ACT II

Cue 5	Evelyn: "Go, go—dispatch." *King's speech heard on radio (BBC Record REJ 187—"50 Years of Royal Broadcasts"*	(Page 35)
Cue 6	Radio "... decision I have made ..." *Telephone rings*	(Page 35)
Cue 7	Evelyn switches radio off *Cut radio speech*	(Page 35)
Cue 8	Powell and Evelyn move to kitchen *Crashing and shot in kitchen*	(Page 37)
Cue 9	Powell: "I've killed another one!" *Telephone rings as per script*	(Page 37)
Cue 10	As main lights go out *Start snow effect outside window*	(Page 44)